# SPRING AND

# PORT WINE

# Bill Naughton

Introduction and questions by
Tim Bezant

Heinemann Educational Publishers
Halley Court, Jordan Hill, Oxford OX2 8EJ
a division of Reed Educational & Professional Publishing Ltd
OXFORD   MELBOURNE   AUCKLAND
JOHANNESBURG   BLANTYRE   GABORONE
IBADAN   PORTSMOUTH (NH) USA   CHICAGO

First published in 1958
First published in the *Hereford Plays* series by Heinemann Educational 1973
First published in the *Heinemann Plays* series 1994
   2000 10 9 8 7 6

A catalogue record for this book is available from the British Library on request.
ISBN 0 435 23304 1

Cover design by Keith Pointing

Design by Jeffrey White Creative Associates

Typeset by Taurus Graphics, Kidlington, Oxon

Printed by Clays Ltd, St Ives plc

# CONTENTS

# PREFACE

In this edition of *Spring and Port Wine*, you will find notes, questions and activities to help in studying the play in class, particularly at GCSE level.

The introduction provides background information on the author, from his birth in Ireland, his Lancashire upbringing and the start of his literary career during World War II. It lists his other publications and examines in detail the play's plot and performance.

The activities at the end of the book range from straightforward *Keeping Track* questions which can be tackled at the end of each act to focus close attention on what is happening in the play, through more detailed work on characters and themes in *Explorations*, to more advanced discussion questions under *Criticism*.

If you are already using the Hereford edition of *Spring and Port Wine*, you will find that the page numbering in the actual playscript is the same, allowing the two editions to be easily used side by side.

# INTRODUCTION

*Bill Naughton*

Bill Naughton was born on 12 June 1910 in Ballyhaunis, County Mayo, Ireland, but was brought to England by his parents when they moved to Bolton, Lancashire in 1914, where his father worked as a miner. Upon leaving school, Naughton worked in a variety of jobs as a weaver, labourer, coal heaver and lorry driver. His experiences of growing up in Bolton are recorded in his autobiography *On the Pig's Back*.

With the outbreak of World War II, he refused to be conscripted to fight, becoming instead a conscientious objector. Moving to London to work, he was first published in 1943 when the London Evening Standard printed one of his short stories. This was followed by a volume of autobiography *A Roof over your Head* in 1945 and his first novel *Rafe Granite* in 1947. Throughout this period, Naughton was also writing short stories for BBC Radio who also first broadcast, in 1957, his play *My Flesh, My Blood*.

By now Naughton was well established as a full-time author, writing novels and short stories for children such as *Late Night on Watling Street* and *The Goalkeeper's Revenge*, plays for both radio and television and finally, in 1963, for the stage, when his play *All in Good Time* was produced. This was followed by *Alfie*, an adaptation of an earlier radio play about a cockney charmer (which was later filmed starring Michael Caine) and, in 1965, by *Spring and Port Wine*.

*Spring and Port Wine* is a revision of his earlier radio play, *My Flesh, My Blood*. After an initial production in Birmingham, it was produced at the Mermaid Theatre, London, from where it subsequently transferred to the

Apollo Theatre in London's West End in 1966. Set in the Bolton with which Naughton was most familiar, the play focuses upon the Crompton family and their close-knit, almost claustrophobic relationships, all of which centre around the father, Rafe. The success of the play led to it being filmed in 1970, starring James Mason as Rafe.

Naughton continued to write throughout the 1970s, further chronicling the adventures of his best-known character in the novel *Alfie Darling*, and writing novels for children (*My Pal Spadger*, *A Dog called Nelson*). Living on the Isle of Man, he came to reflect upon his early life in Bolton in *On the Pig's Back*, which he subtitled 'An Autobiographical Excursion' (1987). He died at his home in January 1992, just before *Spring and Port Wine* was staged again in his adopted home town at Bolton's Octagon Theatre.

His work is distinguished by its attention to detail: detail of characterisation and characters, with whom he refused to sympathise or identify, preferring to allow them to stand on their own two feet before an audience; detail of relationships, which are truthfully and realistically presented in dialogue and action which are deceptively well-crafted; and detail of setting, both historical and geographical, which provide both a believable and realistic background in which his characters interact. It is these qualities which have made *Spring and Port Wine* endure, both on the page and on the stage.

### Spring and Port Wine

When *Spring and Port Wine* was first produced in 1965, drama in Britain had only recently undergone a rebirth which had started in 1956. Before then, plays largely featured middle- or upper-class characters and their lives and concerns. In the late 1950s and early 1960s a wealth of new talent emerged onto the stage, breaking the ground rules which had previously held sway, and Naughton, writing about working-class characters and their relationships and placing his plays in recognisably realistic settings, certainly benefited from this development.

The play is concentrated in its nature: it has just two acts, which in turn show the events over just four days in a single, realistically described semi-detached house in Bolton. Furthermore, the action is concentrated upon a single family (Rafe Crompton, aged about fifty and the head of the family, his wife Daisy who is in her forties, and their adult children: Florence, Harold, Hilda and Wilfred, all of whom still live at home with their parents), the young man who hopes to marry into that family, and their immediate neighbour. Finally, the action of the play presents the climax of a period of the Cromptons' family life, for the events that unfold have clearly been brewing for a very long time.

Rafe Crompton is described as 'a man very much himself' and 'quietly sure of himself'. While he is not stern or overbearing with his wife and children, his are the standards by which the family still lives. While he does not explicitly impose those standards, he makes no secret of them and it is clear that Hilda and Harold at least are starting to question them, if not yet to their father's face. It is only when Hilda refuses the herring for her Friday tea that matters start to come to a head and Rafe, determined not to be beaten by his daughter, determines to ensure that she eats it as intended.

It is this conflict of wills which forms the main plot of the play. Hilda is as strong-willed as her father, who is moved to reflect that 'the apple doesn't fall far from the tree'. Yet while she lives in her father's house, she has to live by his standards. After two days of family tension she decides to eat the herring, 'skin, tail, fins' – 'the lot', but only in order to prove herself to her father. That she is unable to do so, is due to matters beyond her control, but in the aftermath, furious with her father, she single-mindedly decides to leave home, there and then, never to return to 'this rotten prison'.

Her older sister, Florence, is similarly forced to a decision, yet for her one that is much harder, for she admires her father so much more. When Arthur, her boyfriend, proposes marriage to her so that they might both benefit from his promotion, her loyalty to her future husband overcomes her loyalty to her father. Despite Rafe's warnings of the consequences she too leaves the family home with Arthur, who as an outsider, has no qualms in telling Rafe exactly what he thinks of him.

Harold and Wilfred, the sons of the family, initially lack their sisters' determination. Harold complains about his father's attitudes behind his back and is a nagging thorn in his side, but rather than confronting Rafe he attempts to maintain a detached and superior attitude, frequently expressed through his sense of humour. Wilfred, however, who is the baby of the family, is driven to confront Rafe, for it is he who attempts to resolve Hilda's problem by giving her herring to the family's cat. In the subsequent inquest into the truth, Wilfred denies that he did so: when he collapses with one of his 'turns'. On coming round, he confesses his guilt, but now both sons' frustration has come to a head and both resolve to leave home too.

Daisy, Rafe's wife, is immediately caught up in this family conflict but is also immediately overruled. She, however, has problems of her own, in ensuring that the housekeeping money is kept to her husband's high standards and in ensuring that she gets back the money she has lent to their neighbour, Betsy Jane. As Betsy Jane repeatedly fails to pay her debt to Daisy, she in turn is driven to desperate measures in order to make good the housekeeping, allowing Betsy Jane to pawn Rafe's new coat. The fact that Daisy feels that she has to keep her feelings to herself, only makes her situation worse as she starts to see her family disintegrate around her.

That so much family conflict is brought to an acceptably harmonious resolution is largely due to Rafe's strength of character. When he discovers that his new overcoat is missing, he is moved to comfort Daisy in her distress at what has happened rather than to chastise her. This in turn prompts him to reveal to her and to the audience the true depth of his feelings for his family, and roots of and reasons for those feelings in his own hard upbringing. Rather than attempt to bully his children into doing as he wishes, he allows them the opportunity to make up their own minds about their futures, confesses that he too feels wearied by family life and insists that there are to be no more secrets kept from one another. A tragic disintegration of the family is avoided, and it is clear at the end of the play that the family, even allowing for Florence's marriage, will remain a close-knit unit. If the conclusion of the play appears to be contrived or sentimental as a 'happy ending', the reasons for the characters' decisions about their futures are all believable within the context of the play.

## In Performance

In preparing the production of *Spring and Port Wine* at Bolton's Octagon Theatre in 1992, director Lawrence Till found the play to be vivid in the way it evokes a sense of the period in which it was written. It is clearly a play of its place and time: the work, customs and social background referred to in the text are specific to mid-Lancashire in the mid 1960s and any attempt to update the play would necessitate wholesale and consequently destructive rewriting. Similarly, he found the characters to be very clear and direct. While some of their relationships and attitudes may now appear to be dated, their motivations, interaction and the nature of the issues raised by their interaction are timeless.

The detail implicit in Naughton's work has already been noted. Clearly, a successful production of the play would require a detailed and realistic set of the 'living-room, kitchen and scullery of the Crompton home', with furniture, props, decoration and set dressing carefully selected to convey the nature and background of the family that lives in this 'comfortable, prosperous working-class home'.

The action and dialogue of the play is similarly detailed and realistic and the characters would need to be presented to an audience in a similar fashion. An actor portraying Rafe would need to take care not to make him overbearing or self-important, so that when he is moved to bring his standards to bear, he does so in such a manner that is believable and not out of character but is, rather, an extension of his quiet certainty. Only once does he go too far, when he 'obsessively' insists on Wilfred swearing upon the Bible. Whether or not some awareness in Rafe that he had done so would be appropriate in performance would need to be a careful decision for the director and actor to take; is Rafe aware of the extremity of his behaviour and its consequences?

Daisy's initial contentment would need to give way to rising distress and apprehension when the chain of loans and events she has set in motion goes beyond her control. While an actress would need to show the resilience in the character who knows that family arguments will eventually blow themselves out, she would also need to show the increasing discontent, desperation and decisiveness required in Act Two, Scene Two as she attempts to break open the cash-box with Betsy Jane. Similarly, as Rafe discovers that his overcoat is missing, the actress playing Daisy would need to convey her distress in a believable manner, avoiding melodrama and arousing a degree of sympathy in the audience.

Hilda is described as 'fresh and gay'; in Act Two, Scene

Three Rafe mentions her moods. Clearly she is changeable in nature, which accounts for her refusal of the herring. Her strong-willed nature has also been noted. The fact that she may also be pregnant, although she does not yet know it, may also affect the character and might be a factor in the actress's performance of the character. Certainly, an actress would need to convey Hilda's liveliness, strength, stubbornness, unhappiness and, ultimately, relief at her imminent reconciliation with her father at the very end of the play.

Florence is similarly strong, but in sympathy with her father's attitudes. When faced with the choice of whether to marry Arthur, the nature and depth of the dilemma that this presents to the character would need to be clearly conveyed in the actress's reactions, as would her sudden absolute decisiveness (and her awareness of its implications) when she chooses to leave with Arthur at the end of Act Two, Scene One. She too, however, is happier and reconciled to her father at the end of the play, and an actress would convey this accordingly.

While Harold chafes at the restraint of his father's attitudes, it is expressed through wry humour which would be amusing to an audience. An actor would need to communicate the detached superior attitude from which this humour arises, as well as the character's increasingly simmering discontent. Wilfred tends to live in his brother's shadow, is also given to discontent but has the weakness under pressure which causes him to pass out. An actor would need to show that Wilfred's is a more good-natured character, but neither of the actors playing Harold or Wilfred should show the strength of character required of the actresses playing Hilda and Florence.

The character of Arthur, by comparison, does have the strength to tell Rafe some home truths. Arthur would also need to be shown as sympathetic when comforting Hilda and, of course, both serious and intent in his love for and proposal to Florence. Betsy Jane, the 'neighbourly slattern', is more of a stereotypical character, serving to set Daisy's chain of loans in motion and to reveal what people say about the Cromptons behind their backs. An actress would need to disguise the relatively functional nature of the character by highlighting those aspects of the character which distinguish her from the Crompton family and, crucially, them from her and her type.

The natures and interaction of the members of the Crompton family are clearly established in Act One through Naughton's believable and realistic dialogue. In performance, this dialogue would need to be supplemented and augmented by appropriate action and reaction from the company of actors that would reveal the close-knit nature of the family. It would be vital, in a successful production, that this detailed sense of family feeling should be communicated to the audience so that, when events take their more serious turn, the effects not only on the individual characters but on the family unit as a whole are also clearly conveyed. This, in turn, would make the final reconciliations and the survival of the family all the more poignant and effective.

Finally, the language and dialogue of the play draw upon the dialect and speech patterns of mid-Lancashire. On the whole it is conversational and straightforward but would require careful and detailed rehearsal in order to show the close-knit nature of the relationships within the Crompton family. A successful production would need to project the appropriate accent in order to further heighten the detailed, realistic and naturalistic nature of the play.

## Reading the Play

All plays are written to be performed or, at the very least, read aloud. This is clearly true of the conversational, realistic dialogue of *Spring and Port Wine*. Through hearing the characters speak, a fuller understanding of their attitudes and opinions, both of themselves and of others, will be formed. From this, an understanding of how the characters might express themselves in physical terms may be formed. Only through an effective reading of the play may an understanding of the various characters' ideas, opinions, attitudes and interactions begin to be developed.

Particular parts of the play lend themselves to detailed study or to reading and rehearsal in small groups. A useful approach is to read aloud first of all to understand the action and the relationships; then explore and experiment with the text in order to discover more depth and understanding of the characters and their developing relationships.

Following the play are two series of questions entitled *Keeping Track* and *Explorations*. *Keeping Track* is intended to help your understanding of the action and the characters as the play develops and can be used when reading the play for the first time. *Explorations* are more demanding questions organised according to character, themes, performance and criticism: they may lead on to coursework assignments or examination practice. All the questions are designed to stimulate knowledge, understanding and, hopefully, enjoyment of the play.

**Tim Bezant**

# Cast of First London Performance

Presented by the Mermaid Theatre Trust and Allan Davies Ltd at the Mermaid Theatre, Puddle Dock on 10 November 1965 with the following cast of characters:

| | |
|---|---|
| DAISY CROMPTON | Ruth Dunning |
| FLORENCE CROMPTON | Jennifer Wilson |
| BETSY JANE | Gretchen Franklin |
| WILFRED CROMPTON | Melvin Hayes |
| HAROLD CROMPTON | John Alderton |
| HILDA CROMPTON | Jan Carey |
| RAFE CROMPTON | Alfred Marks |
| ARTHUR | Ray Mort |

The play directed by ALLAN DAVIS
Setting by ADRIAN VAUX

The play was subsequently presented by Allan Davies Ltd, Michael Medwin (for Memorial Enterprises) and the Mermaid Theatre Trust at the Apollo Theatre, Shaftsbury Avenue on 3 January 1966 with the cast unchanged and a setting designed by Hutchison Scott.

# List of Characters

DAISY CROMPTON
FLORENCE CROMPTON
BETSY JANE
WILFRED CROMPTON
HAROLD CROMPTON
HILDA CROMPTON
RAFE CROMPTON
ARTHUR

*The action of the play passes in the Crompton home, Bolton, Lancashire*

**ACT ONE**
Friday

**ACT TWO**
Scene One: Sunday
Scene Two: Monday

*The scene is lowered during Scene Two to denote the passing of a few hours*

TIME: *the present*

# SPRING AND PORT WINE

## ACT ONE

*The living-room, kitchen and scullery of the Crompton home.
Early Friday evening.*

*Most of the stage is taken up by the living-room, which has a
bay window down right, a door to the hall up centre and one to
the kitchen up left. The kitchen also has a door in its down stage
wall which leads to the scullery. The scullery extends down left
of the living-room wall, and in its own left wall is the back door
of the house. The front door is off up right of the corridor centre.
The house is a comfortable, prosperous, working-class home.
The furniture is fairly modern, everything is polished and well
cared for. There is nothing cheap or vulgar.*

*When the curtain rises, the living-room is empty, and a
transistor radio is playing on the sideboard.* DAISY CROMPTON
*enters from the kitchen carrying six side plates which she lays
deftly, humming to the music, on the table, giving extra
attention to* RAFE'S *place at the head.* DAISY *is a seemingly
contented housewife in her forties. She waves out of the window
to* FLORENCE, *then picks up her worn leather bag from the
sideboard, switches off the radio and sits, adding up her
accounts and counting money.*

FLORENCE CROMPTON *enters by front door, hangs up her raincoat
in the hall and enters the living-room carrying a briefcase. She
is a teacher, in her twenties, fresh, attractive, brisk and assured
of manner.*

**FLORENCE**  Hello, Mother!

**DAISY**  Hello, Florence. You're home early.

**FLORENCE**  Just my usual time.

**DAISY**  Then I must be behind.

**FLORENCE**  I expect you are. It's nearly five o'clock.

**DAISY**  Ee, and I haven't got my housekeeping book
balanced.

| | |
|---|---|
| **FLORENCE** | You're on the last minute with those accounts every Friday. |
| **DAISY** | I know, love. I keep putting off the final reckoning. What's six pounds seventeen and ninepence-ha'penny and four pounds nine and tenpence-ha'penny? |
| **FLORENCE** | Eleven pounds seven and eightpence. |
| **DAISY** | You've got your father's head for sums. |
| **FLORENCE** | Have I? Thank you. (*She transfers her clutch bag and exercise books from the briefcase to the table.*) |
| **DAISY** | It's still not right. Dash this weekly reckoning up! Florence, you wouldn't just run your eye over these figures for me, love, just to make sure they're okay? |
| **FLORENCE** | (*taking her spectacles from her bag*) It's every week the same. (*She sits and runs her pencil up the row of figures.*) |
| **DAISY** | I've simply got to make them all tally before your dad gets home. You know how he likes everything to be just so. |
| **FLORENCE** | (*adding up quickly*) Ten pounds one and threepence. |
| **DAISY** | That sum has an honest ring. (*She gives some coins to* FLORENCE.) When does school break up, love? |
| **FLORENCE** | For Easter? Next Wednesday. You've a deficit of twenty-six shillings and fivepence on paper. |
| **DAISY** | I can't have. |
| **FLORENCE** | I know – but you have. |
| **DAISY** | I wonder where it all goes! Florence, love, could you advance me a pound until after Dad's given me the housekeeping money? Just to keep his mind at rest. FLORENCE *takes a note out of her bag and hands it to* DAISY. |
| **FLORENCE** | (*disapproving*) One pound. |
| **DAISY** | Ta, love. Don't be surprised if you get home one Friday and I've done a bunk. |
| **FLORENCE** | (*returning the coins*) It's your own fault – you should put down on paper every ... |
| **DAISY** | (*cutting in*) I know – every item as I pay for it! That's what your dad keeps telling me. Well, the money's right, it was only the reckoning that was wrong. |

| | |
|---|---|
| **FLORENCE** | (*returning the notebook and putting away her spectacles*) And that's still not right. You're six and fivepence out. |
| **DAISY** | So I am. Now suppose I'd paid the window-cleaner – which I haven't, because he hasn't been. |
| **FLORENCE** | Mother! |
| **DAISY** | There's nothing dishonest about it. It's just for your dad's peace of mind. (*She takes the notebook and begins to write in it.*) Window-cleaner, eight-and-six. That takes me out of the red, and puts me a couple of bob to the good. Funny, but I can get away with that touch nearly every week. It seems to be his one blind spot. |
| **FLORENCE** | God help you if he ever finds out. |
| **DAISY** | God help him, poor chap, he has such faith in me. Is Arthur coming round tonight? |
| **FLORENCE** | I hope not. I've some marking to do. Three nights a week of Arthur is quite enough. |
| **DAISY** | Once you get married you'll have seven nights a week of him. And not just holding hands in the pictures either! |
| **FLORENCE** | That won't be for some time yet, I hope. |
| **DAISY** | You never know your luck. |
| | BETSY JANE, *a neighbourly slattern, enters by the back door. She is obviously in a hurry. The light starts to fade slowly as dusk falls.* |
| **BETSY JANE** | I say, Daisy! |
| **DAISY** | That you, Betsy Jane? (*She rises and moves up right.*) |
| | BETSY JANE *enters the living-room. She sees* FLORENCE *and her manner changes.* |
| **BETSY JANE** | Hello, Florence. |
| **FLORENCE** | Hello. |
| **BETSY JANE** | (*looking round*) Your mother's got all her week-end cleaning and polishing done – just fancy! |
| **DAISY** | (*laying the table with cutlery from the sideboard*) Aye, Rafe always likes to come home to everything spick and span of a Friday. |
| **BETSY JANE** | He would! But he wouldn't get it from me. (*She sniffs.*) I see you're having herrings for tea. |

| | |
|---|---|
| DAISY | (*setting the jam pot and spoon*) Yes, and they're lovely. Fancy a couple? |
| BETSY JANE | I wouldn't give you a thank-you for all the herring in the North Sea. I'm more partial to sausages or black pudding. Something savoury like. |
| DAISY | Rafe has always liked fish of a Friday. |
| BETSY JANE | I suppose you others have got to like it. |
| FLORENCE | And why shouldn't we? |
| DAISY | Why – what's wrong with a good fresh herring? |
| BETSY JANE | You needn't get up in arms! I only thought it a bit High Church for a chap as were eddicated at Cotton Lane Baptists. 'Course, they do say they're very nutritious. |
| FLORENCE | (*rising and moving up centre*) Really! I'll go and change. |

*A buzzer sounds.*

Now don't get behind, Mother – that's the buzzer.

| | |
|---|---|
| DAISY | (*moving her bag to the sideboard*) No, I'd better not. |
| BETSY JANE | I'll be off in a minute, Florence. I just wanted a word in private with your mum. |

FLORENCE *goes out.* BETSY JANE *cocks a snook.*

Eee, I thought she was never going.

| | |
|---|---|
| DAISY | What's up, Betsy Jane? |
| BETSY JANE | Daisy, I'm in a right mess! Could you let me have five pounds? |
| DAISY | Five pounds! I'm sorry, but ... |
| BETSY JANE | It's the flaming television fella. I'm behind with my payments, and he's just come to take it back if I don't pay five pounds off the arrears. |
| DAISY | You don't mean to say he's in there now? |
| BETSY JANE | Aye, I left the front door on the latch and he caught me. And now he's got it all disconnected ready to take back unless I hand him over five pounds in ready cash. |
| DAISY | You couldn't have come at a worse time. |
| BETSY JANE | Yon chap will murder me if he comes home and finds the telly gone. He thinks I'm straight up with all my payments. |

| | |
|---|---|
| **DAISY** | I'm so sorry ... |
| **BETSY JANE** | And think of the disgrace in front of all my neighbours if they see that fella carrying it out. |
| **DAISY** | I'm sorry, but ... |
| **BETSY JANE** | I swear my oath I'll let you have it back by seven o'clock – as soon as he hands over his money. |
| **DAISY** | Rafe's got this obsession about keeping accounts straight. He likes to start every week afresh. |
| **BETSY JANE** | I wish I could start afresh. |
| **DAISY** | Would two pound ten see you through? (*She opens her bag.*) |
| **BETSY JANE** | He won't budge for under five pounds. I'm sure you could fiddle the other fifty bob one way or another. |
| **DAISY** | The other? I'll have to fiddle for the first. Is there nobody else you could ask? |
| **BETSY JANE** | Is there hell as like! They're all as badly off as me. Do try to wangle the five pounds. |
| **DAISY** | Look, it'll take me all my time to get fifty bob. |
| **BETSY JANE** | Tell him you've paid some bill you haven't. |
| **DAISY** | I wouldn't want to tell a barefaced lie to Rafe. |
| **BETSY JANE** | Why not? Anyway, what right has he to interfere with your housekeeping? That's the wife's job. |
| **DAISY** | So long as all the bills are paid I'm happy running the house. |
| **BETSY JANE** | How can you say you're happy? And how do you run the house? Mony runs the house, and that jumped-up husband of yours handles it all. |
| **DAISY** | Now don't you be so cheeky in my home. Rafe has never seen me short of money and we don't owe a halfpenny. How many wives on this estate could say that? |
| **BETSY JANE** | Well, we owe everybody and I'm always short of money, and the television chap's in possession at the moment, but I've still got something you haven't got. |
| **DAISY** | What's that? What've you got I haven't? |
| **BETSY JANE** | A wife's pride! Aye, and independence. |

DAISY        (*rising*) How dare you say I've no pride!

BETSY JANE   I dare because it's true. They all say it, all your
             neighbours. They're always talking about you and
             him and his domineering ways.

DAISY        (*shocked*) You mean my neighbours talk about me
             behind my back?

BETSY JANE   Yes, they do.

DAISY        I don't believe it.

             WILFRED CROMPTON *enters by the back door. He is
             eighteen but looks younger. He is wearing a factory
             mechanic's blue overalls and a cap. During the
             following speech he removes these and hangs them
             on a peg on the door.*

BETSY JANE   Don't you! Why Mrs Clegg was only saying the
             other day what she'd do if a man dared attempt to
             run her side of the home. He might manage to have
             everything paid up, he might manage to keep the
             house in order, but in doing it he's sucked all the
             pride out of you. You talk about not telling him a
             lie – why, your whole life is a flaming lie, if you ask
             me. How can a man run a home? That's the
             woman's job, always has been. A man has no right
             to attempt it. It's not natural.

             WILFRED *enters the living-room.*

WILFRED      What's not natural?

BETSY JANE   (*with a snort*) Oh, go to hell!

             BETSY JANE *goes to the kitchen with a look at* DAISY,
             *then goes out by the back door.*

WILFRED      What the heck's up with her? (*Noticing that* DAISY *is
             upset.*) Has something upset you, Mum?

DAISY        Listen, Wilf, would you say I had no pride?

WILFRED      No pride – you, Mum! Who dare say that? (*He kisses
             her.*) You've pride in everything you touch.

DAISY        (*unconvinced*) Bless you, lad. Call her back.

             WILFRED *hurries to the back door and whistles.*

WILFRED      Hi! Betsy Jane! Come back; my mum wants you.

             DAISY *goes into the kitchen and then to the back door.*
             What was up with her?

DAISY   Could you let me have five pounds, love, out of your wages?

WILFRED   Five pounds! Aye, I expect I could at a pinch. (*He takes out his wage packet and extracts notes.*) It might throw me a bit short for when I'm paying over to Dad.

DAISY   I'll get a couple of pounds off our Harold for you – just to tide you over.

WILFRED   Good. I say, you're not lending it to Betsy Jane, are you?

DAISY   It's all right. She's got some trouble. You won't let your father know?

WILFRED   What he doesn't know won't keep him awake. But I don't trust her.

BETSY JANE, *shamefaced, enters the back door.* WILFRED *picks up the cat from outside and takes it into the living-room.*

BETSY JANE   What is it, Daisy?

DAISY   Here, your five pound. I got it off our Wilf. Get in home before it's too late.

BETSY JANE   Ee, no thanks – I can't take it – not after what I said to you.

DAISY   Let's say no more about it.

BETSY JANE   (*briskly*) Ta then. You're a good neighbour, Daisy. It's terrible when you've nobody to turn to. I'll let you have it back the minute yon chap hands over his money to me. He's never later than seven. I hope I can do as much for you one day.

*She turns to go.*

DAISY   Hey, I say ...

BETSY JANE *turns back.*

Do they – do my neighbours really talk about me in that way?

BETSY JANE   Eh? Now don't take what I said to heart.

DAISY   I'm asking you.

BETSY JANE   Not really. I think it's only jealousy. They all envy you your nice home. You know how they are – don't like to see anybody better off than themselves. Try to forget what I said.

BETSY JANE *hurries off.* DAISY *wipes her eye and returns slowly to the living-room.*

**WILFRED**   Has anything upset you, Mum?

**DAISY**   I've just heard a bit of truth, love – it can be upsetting.

**WILFRED**   Take no notice of what she says.

**DAISY**   I'll go and wash me.

**WILFRED**   And I'll grab the sink while I've a chance.

DAISY *goes out.* WILFRED *takes the cat to the kitchen , then enters the scullery, switching on the light.* HAROLD CROMPTON *enters through the back door, whistling. He is in his twenties and has a dry, comical air. He works in a spinning mill and wears corduroy trousers and bicycle clips, a cardigan, cap and scarf)*
Howgo, Harold!

**HAROLD**   Howgo, squire!

WILFRED *throws a towel over his shoulders and washes his face and hands at the sink.* HAROLD *hangs up his scarf and takes off his clips.*

**WILFRED**   You can come and have a sluice here in a minute.

**HAROLD**   (*taking the towel and wiping his hands*) I don't need to wash me. We're working on Egyptians – beautiful cotton – spins like silk. How come our Hilda's not home with you?

**WILFRED**   They were having a bit of a do over in the weaving shed. Some chap getting wed.

**HAROLD**   There's one born every minute. (*He goes into the living-room and sits in armchair with his feet up.*)

**WILFRED**   No, there's always a big rush before Easter to save the income tax.

**HAROLD**   I'll bet that's not the only reason they're rushing. (*He takes out a cigarette and lights it.*)

**WILFRED**   (*moving into the living-room*) Why – what other?

**HAROLD**   (*throwing the towel at* WILFRED) Skip it, son.

**WILFRED**   Hey, you mucky beggar, look what a mess you've made of this towel.

**HAROLD**   Don't worry. I'll send you to the launderette with it in the morning.

FLORENCE *enters, switching on the pendant and desk lamp by the switch at the door.*

**WILFRED**      Some hopes you've got! Hello, Flo!

**FLORENCE**     Hello, love.

**HAROLD**       (*in a posh voice*) Hello, Flo. Where's Mum?

**WILFRED**      Having a wash in t'bathroom. (*Drying his face and buttoning his cuffs.*) Hi, that reminds me, you've got to give me a couple of quid.

**HAROLD**       I have! What for?

**WILFRED**      Mum'll tell you. She's been lending money.

**HAROLD**       Keep me out of your mother's troubles. I'm very short myself this week – I backed a few losers.

**FLORENCE**     (*moving to the fire, pushing* HAROLD'S *feet aside to get the coal glove*) Can't you keep your big feet out of the way?

**HAROLD**       Do you call twelve-and-a-halfs big? The old man takes fifteens.

**FLORENCE**     (*putting coal on the fire*) If you mean your father say your father.

**HAROLD**       I don't. I mean the old man, old Crompton. Ever heard of him?

**FLORENCE**     I'd like to see you if he comes in and catches you in his chair – and stinking the room with your fags.

**HAROLD**       That little word 'if'.

**WILFRED**      (*putting on his jacket and combing his hair*) Better get the Airwick spray out, mate, or he'll smell you've been smoking.

**HAROLD**       I don't care what he smells. Let him come to me if he has any complaints – and I'll tell him where he gets off.

                 FLORENCE *goes to the sideboard and then sets the napkins on the table.*

**WILFRED**      Don't forget tonight's his monthly union meeting. So don't you set him off.

                 WILFRED *goes to the kitchen with the towel.*

**HAROLD**       I should worry! No wonder the union secretary ended up where he did.

                 HILDA CROMPTON *runs in from the front door and*

*enters the sitting-room. She is aged nineteen and is a weaver at the mills. She is fresh and gay. She carries a shoulder-bag and 'Weekend' magazine, and wears a bright raincoat.*

HILDA       Oh, I have had a good time! (*She moves to the piano.*)

HAROLD      Be careful your dad doesn't hear you.

HILDA       He's not home yet?

FLORENCE    Of course not. It's not Dad's time yet.

HILDA       Thank heaven. Where's Mum? (*She takes off her raincoat and leaves her things on the piano-stool.*)

HAROLD      (*cutting in*) She's run off with Co-op coal chap – they've made off for Blackpool with his week's takings.

HILDA *pushes* HAROLD'S *cap over his eyes.* HAROLD *takes it off.*

DAISY *enters, smiling.*

DAISY       Here I am, love. Ee, you do look bonny. (*She hugs Hilda.*)

HILDA       Ee, we have had a good time, Mum! We've had a lovely footing.

DAISY       Yes, love – you look it. Straighten your hair.

FLORENCE    You've had a what?

HAROLD      (*mimicking*) A party – where all foot their share.

HILDA       (*looking in the mirror*) Yes – our mechanic's getting married tomorrow, so all the weavers in our shed pooled seven-and-six apiece for a cheese and wine party. It was lovely.

DAISY       Ee, we only had cider and sausage rolls in my time.

HAROLD      Aye, things were tight during the Boer War.

HILDA       Smell my breath, Mum! I'd about three glassfuls of port.

HAROLD      I can smell it from here. Springtime orgies in the weaving shed.

WILFRED *enters from the kitchen.*

HILDA       Wilf, love, could you hear us singing hymns after?

FLORENCE    Hymns on top of that lot!

FLORENCE *snorts and exits to the kitchen.*

WILFRED     Aye, we could even hear you in the mechanics' shop with the lathe going. (*He plays the piano.*)

HILDA, DAISY *and* WILFRED *sing. As they do so,* HILDA

*picks up her things and* HAROLD'S *cap. She puts her
bag and the cap on the piano, hangs her mac up in
the hall, and returns with the magazine.* DAISY *sets
the cruet and sugar on the table.*

**HILDA**
**DAISY**   } (*singing*) { Follow, follow, I will follow Jesus.
**WILFRED**              Anywhere, everywhere, I will follow on.

**HAROLD**   Funny choice for a party piece.

**HILDA**
**DAISY**   } (*singing*) Follow, follow, I will follow Jesus.
**WILFRED**

**HAROLD**   Hey, Daisy, cut out the yodelling. I'm starving.

**HILDA**
**DAISY**   } (*singing*) Anywhere He leads, I will follow on.
**WILFRED**

*They stop singing, and* WILFRED *turns and whispers to*
DAISY.

**DAISY**   Harold, love, give our Wilf two pounds for me.

**HAROLD**   What for?

**DAISY**   I'll let you have it back later when Betsy Jane settles
up with me.

**HAROLD**   You've been lending that one money? You want
your head examining.

HILDA *moves to the desk.*

**WILFRED**   Come on, hand over ...

**DAISY**   It's for my sake.

**HAROLD**   All right – I'll do it for you, Mum.

HAROLD *reluctantly gives* WILFRED *two pounds.* HILDA
*looks at the letters on the desk.* DAISY *watches her.*
(*To* WILFRED) Don't forget I want it back, mate.

**WILFRED**   I don't owe it to you.

**DAISY**   I'm afraid there's no letter for you, love.

**HILDA**   It's all right.

**HAROLD**   He's forgot you, girl.

**HILDA**   Who?

**HAROLD**   As if you didn't know! Start frying them herrings,
Mum.

FLORENCE *enters with two plates of bread and butter.*
HAROLD *rises, takes a slice, and sits again putting his feet up.* HILDA *sits.* FLORENCE *puts the plates on the table.*

**HILDA**  Who said herrings? Don't say we're having herrings!

**WILFRED**  I thought you liked them.

**HAROLD**  So did I!

**HILDA**  Well, I've gone off 'em.

**DAISY**  That's funny.

**HILDA**  What's funny?

**DAISY**  Nothing.

**HAROLD**  She is getting above herself.

**DAISY**  Your dad asked for them special.

DAISY *looks at* HILDA *and exits to the kitchen.*

**FLORENCE**  (*drawing the curtains*) And what's wrong with herrings?

**HILDA**  I don't know – I've just gone off 'em.

**HAROLD**  Well, they don't go with port wine.

**DAISY**  (*off*) Hey – Wilf! Come and get your cat from under my feet, and put him outside.

**WILFRED**  Coming, Mum. They say they're brain food, you know.

WILFRED *goes to the kitchen.*

**HAROLD**  Then you'd better eat our Hilda's.

**HILDA**  The thought of them puts me off.

**HAROLD**  (*in a lady-like voice*) Do they repeat on you, deah? (*He belches.*)

**HILDA**  (*rising miserably*) I don't know how it is – but I've only to smell 'em these days ... (*She hits* HAROLD'S *feet, crosses to the standard lamp, switches it on, then sits on the sofa and reads her magazine.*)

**HAROLD**  I've noticed you're getting a bit fussy. Mind you, I wouldn't object to fillet steak for a change, and a bottle of vintage Beaujolais. But what puts me off is waiting. Why do we always have to wait for him for our tea? Who does he think he is?

WILFRED *enters the scullery from the kitchen with the cat and a saucer and goes out through the back door.*

**FLORENCE** (*moving to* HAROLD) What else would we do?

**HAROLD** (*rising*) What I say is let's all sit down and start tea right now. First come first served. Come on – who's game?

**FLORENCE** I'd like to see the day when you dare.

WILFRED *rushes in through the back door and round into the living-room.*

**HAROLD** (*sitting again*) Well, if he says anything to me I'll send him about his business. I've stood just about enough of his old guff. After all, we are living in a democracy, you know.

**WILFRED** (*tapping* HAROLD'S *shoulder*) He's just turned the top of the crescent.

**HAROLD** (*casually*) Who do you think you're kidding? (*With alarm.*) He's not, has he? (*He rises.*) The old man ...?

FLORENCE *exits to the kitchen.* DAISY *enters with tartare sauce and moves to the table.*

(*Agitatedly flapping a paper about.*) Here, help me. Waft this smoke about. Come on, quick. (*He stubs out his cigarette in the coal scuttle.*) Get going! Turn the telly on; it'll take his mind off things.

DAISY, *with calm assurance, tidies the easy chair.* WILFRED *turns on the television.*

Hey, Mum, can you smell the smoke?

**DAISY** I'll start putting the herrings on; that'll kill it.

*The television sound and light flicker come on.* DAISY *exits to the kitchen, switching on the light. After finally wafting the smoke away,* HAROLD *joins* WILFRED *watching the television, which becomes noisy.* RAFE CROMPTON *enters from the front door. He has a solid, fatherly look and is a man very much himself. He is a cotton-mill worker, aged about fifty. There is nothing grim or stern about him – he is just quietly sure of himself. He hangs up his cap in the hall then enters the living-room. He has with him his thermos,*

*lunch-box, and copy of the evening paper. He walks*
*quietly across to the television set and switches it off.*

**RAFE** I don't think we need that on.... Listen to the silence.
(*He listens.*) Just feel how soothing a bit of quiet is.
(*He throws the newspaper into his armchair.*)

**WILFRED** I thought it would liven things up, Dad.

**HAROLD** Aye, that's right.

**RAFE** I don't need livening up. You two might, but I don't.
What I need after my day's work is a bit of peace.

*DAISY enters, moves to RAFE, kisses him, then takes his*
*thermos and lunch-box.*

**DAISY** Hello, Dad.

**RAFE** 'Mother.

**DAISY** Had a hard day?

**RAFE** (*taking off his jacket*) The work in the engine shed
is not nearly as hard as it used to be, but somehow
it's more wearing.

**DAISY** (*putting RAFE's jacket on the back of his chair*) I
expect it begins to tell on you by the week-end.
Tea'll be ready soon.

**RAFE** Good.

(*DAISY goes into the kitchen.*)

(*sniffing.*) Have you been smoking those fags again?
(*HAROLD shakes his head, then coughs.*)
Just before your meal. When will you learn some
sense? (*He opens the window. To HILDA.*) Hello, love.

**HILDA** Hello, Dad.

**RAFE** (*sniffing and looking at HILDA*) Funny, I thought I
could smell drink.

**HILDA** We had a party in the mill, and I had some port
wine.

**RAFE** You know what they say – wine is a turncoat –
starts off as a friend and then turns into an enemy.

**HILDA** I didn't reach that stage.

**RAFE** (*reading a headline over HILDA's shoulder*) 'What
happened after the dance. Teenagers' night of sex
and drugs.' Do you have to waste your money on
such trash?

| | |
|---|---|
| **HILDA** | I didn't buy it. Betty Partington gave it to me. |
| **RAFE** | But why fill your mind with that muck? |
| **HILDA** | It's the truth, after all. |
| **WILFRED** | Aye, there's that to it, Dad. |
| **HAROLD** | You've got to face facts in this life. |
| **RAFE** | (*moving the piano*) Nay, it might be news, but it's never truth. (*He picks up the family Bible.*) You may question every fact in this holy book – but who dare say every word isn't God's truth! |

FLORENCE *enters carrying* RAFE'S *slippers.*

| | |
|---|---|
| **FLORENCE** | Here are your slippers, Dad. |
| **RAFE** | Thank you, Florence. (*He takes a book from the number on the piano – 'A Book of Sixteenth Century Verse'.*) Truth is a spiritual thing, it survives the centuries, whereas the chap who wrote that filth had only one thing in mind – to sell his rotten magazines. It's their trade, see. Now listen to this – this is what I call truth. |

FLORENCE *sits on the piano stool to listen.* HAROLD *mimes the words in time with* RAFE.

'When I do count the clock that tells the time,
And see the brave day sunk in hideous night;
When I behold the violet past prime,
And sable curls all silvered o'er with white;
When lofty trees I see barren of leaves,
Which ...' (*He raises his head and loses the place.*)

| | |
|---|---|
| **HAROLD** | 'Which erst from heat did canopy the herd!' |
| **RAFE** | Thank you very much. (*He replaces the book and puts his slippers on.*) I only hope they take me away in my wooden box when I fail to be stirred by such beauty. |
| **HILDA** | Folk would think you were daft if you walked about with a book of poetry under your arm. |
| **RAFE** | Who cares what folk think? I don't. If most folk were to know what other folk thought about them, they'd drop dead with shock. |
| **HAROLD** | Some would – that's for sure! |

| | |
|---|---|
| FLORENCE | (*moving to her handbag and taking out money*) Dad, before I forget, I went to the bank in the lunch hour. Here's my week's money. Will you take it now? |
| RAFE | I might as well get it over with. Just a tick. I've a good idea what a lot of folk think I am. |
| HAROLD | You can't stop them from thinking. |

HILDA *rises.* WILFRED, HAROLD *and* HILDA *begin to take money from their wage packets with varying reluctance and secrecy.* RAFE *crosses to the desk, takes a key from his pocket, opens the desk and takes out a small security box which he unlocks and opens. He takes a wage packet from his pocket, picks up a long paper-knife, slits the packet open, and puts some notes in the security box. He then takes* FLORENCE'S *money.*

| | |
|---|---|
| RAFE | Thank you. |

HILDA *puts a five-pound note on the desk in an offhand manner and returns to the sofa.*
Thank you.
FLORENCE *picks up* RAFE'S *boots and goes into the kitchen.*

| | |
|---|---|
| WILFRED | Here's my bagging money, Dad. (*He hands over five pounds.*) |
| | You'll find that right, I think. |

DAISY *enters with a butter-dish which she places on the table. She then returns to the kitchen.*

| | |
|---|---|
| RAFE | (*in the manner of a bank clerk, with no interest in money as such*) Thank you. |

WILFRED *moves away.*

| | |
|---|---|
| HAROLD | (*hurriedly*) Here y'are, Dad ... |
| RAFE | Thank you ... |

RAFE *never counts, but he knows.*
Hey, what's this?

| | |
|---|---|
| HAROLD | Eh? Eh – what's what? |
| RAFE | You're a pound short. |
| HAROLD | (*too quickly*) Eh? Oh, sorry, Dad – sorry. (*He takes a pound note out of his pocket.*) |
| RAFE | I'm not one of them, lad. (*Calling.*) Mother! |
| HAROLD | One of what? |

RAFE    You know - one of them you seem to take me for!
        (*He takes a note.*)
        DAISY *enters from the kitchen with a trolley loaded
        with the tea things.*

DAISY   Tea's ready, everybody. Yes, Dad?
        HAROLD *takes his plate off the trolley and sits at the
        table.*

        WILFRED *helps* DAISY *to lay the rest of the plates.*

RAFE    How did you manage this week with your
        housekeeping money, Mother?

DAISY   Oh, I've a bit left. You'll see it there.

RAFE    (*putting the housekeeping money out on the desk
        and locking the cash-box*) Did it work out right on
        paper – I mean in figures?

DAISY   I think so – near enough.

RAFE    Just let me see it, Mother – just to cast an eye over it.

DAISY   It's there, in my bag. (*She indicates the sideboard.*)
        RAFE *opens* DAISY'S *bag and takes out the notebook.*

RAFE    By gum, the price of meat these days – no wonder
        yon butcher drives round in a Jag. I see the
        window-cleaner was round again. Fair enough,
        Mother, you're even a shilling or two to the good
        according to my reckoning. I'll make a chartered
        accountant of you yet. (*He puts the housekeeping
        money in the book and locks the desk.*)

DAISY   Don't aim too high, Dad.

RAFE    You're doing very well, Mother. At times you
        astonish me.

DAISY   At times I astonish myself.

RAFE    (*taking off his collar and tie and crossing to the
        table*) But always take care of the pence...

HAROLD  (*aside*) And he'll take care of the pounds!
        *We are never sure whether* RAFE *hears.*

RAFE    (*holding out the book and money*) Here's your next
        week's money, Mother. Don't stint yourself, and let
        me know if you're running short.

DAISY   Will you put it down by my handbag. Come on to
        your tea, now.

RAFE    (*putting the money, book, collar and tie on the sideboard*) You should always check it. Even from me! I'll go and rinse my hands first. Money can be a good servant – but a very poor master. So always have it right.

*RAFE goes out. As soon as the door is closed,* HAROLD *lets out a raspberry.*

DAISY    Harold! (*She taps him on the shoulder as she goes to the sideboard to sort out the money.*)

*FLORENCE enters from the kitchen with the teapot. She switches off the kitchen light and takes the pot to the trolley.*

WILFRED    You didn't get away with it, did you?

HAROLD    Away with what? Oh, you mean the quid short? It was a genuine mistake.

WILFRED    You can't get past him.

HAROLD    Him – I could get that feller down with chicken feed. Hey, Daisy, let's get cracking. I'm famished.

FLORENCE    You'll wait until your father takes his place.

HAROLD    Who says I will? (*He grabs a slice of bread and butter.*)

FLORENCE    (*slapping his hand*) You greedy beggar. Don't let Dad catch you slancing.

HAROLD    I don't care what he catches me at!

DAISY    Come on, Hilda love, sit in.

HILDA    I'm not that hungry.

HAROLD    No, but we are. Come on.

*HILDA hesitates, then slowly walks to her place, at the table.*

*WILFRED moves to his place, below* HAROLD. DAISY *regards the table, which is now laid.*

DAISY    Oh, Florence, before I forget I must give you that pound you lent me.

WILFRED    You're doing a lot of money juggling, Mum.

DAISY    Ssh! (*She takes a note and hands it to Florence.*) Ta very much.

FLORENCE    Oh, thanks, Mother. (*She takes the note.*)

*RAFE enters spotting* DAISY'S *guilty movement. They all sit down to tea:* RAFE *is at the head of the table,*

FLORENCE *left of him, and* HAROLD *on his right.* WILFRED
*sits on* HAROLD'S *right, and* DAISY *below* HAROLD. HILDA
*is down left of* FLORENCE, *where she is conspicuous to
the audience.*

**RAFE**       What was that, Mother?

**DAISY**      A little something I borrowed off our Florence.

**RAFE**       (*quoting*) 'Neither a borrower nor a lender be ...'

**HAROLD**     Hey, Wilf, pass the tartar sauce.

**WILFRED**    The what?

**FLORENCE**   Sauce tartare. (*She picks it up.*) Here you are.

**HAROLD**     Ta ta. 'For loan oft loses both itself and friend.' Do
               you fancy some, Dad?

**RAFE**       I prefer the natural taste of the herring.

**HAROLD**     I find this sauce quite piquant. How much a jar is it,
               Mum?

**DAISY**      I don't know – oh, one-and-ninepence. I knew
               there was something I didn't write down. ( *She starts
               to rise, then sits.*) I'll do it later.
               RAFE *looks at her.*

**HAROLD**     What about you, Florence?

**FLORENCE**   I'll give it a miss. These taste lovely as they are.

**HILDA**      I say, Mum, I really don't fancy my herring – if you
               don't mind.

**DAISY**      No, of course not, love! What would you like
               instead? I've got some nice fresh eggs.

**HAROLD**     Aye, with some streaky rashers.

**HILDA**      No, just an egg.

**HAROLD**     Sunny side up?

**HILDA**      Done on both sides. But wait till you're finished,
               Mum.

**DAISY**      It's all right, love – won't take me a minute. (*Rising.*)
               You must be ready for it after a day's work ...
               *They think they have got away with it, but* RAFE
               *quietly beckons* DAISY *to sit.*

**RAFE**       Hold on a minute, Mother. (*To* HILDA.) Is there
               something wrong with your herring?

**HILDA**      No, nothing wrong with it – only I don't feel like it.

RAFE That's a lovely fresh herring, it's been done in best butter, and yet you have the nerve to sit there and say you don't feel like it.

HILDA What else can I say if I don't?

RAFE You can eat it and say nothing.

HAROLD Well, that's asking a bit much, Dad.

HILDA I'll just go and fry myself an egg, Mum.

RAFE No, you won't.

HILDA Why not?

RAFE Because this is a home, not a cafeteria.

HILDA I'm entitled to some choice over what I have for my tea – I'm bringing my share of the money into the home.

RAFE You don't think I thought less of you over all the years you never brought in a ha'penny? I'd as soon see the smiling face you had in them days than you were bringing twenty pounds a week home today.

WILFRED Here, Dad, to save any bother, I'll eat our Hilda's herring.

RAFE You'll do nothing of the sort. You get on with your own tea.

DAISY (*not put out*) Dad - it wouldn't take a second to fry an egg.

RAFE There's no fried eggs coming on the scene.

HILDA Then there's no point in my waiting here. (*Rising.*) Excuse me, everybody – I'll just go upstairs...

RAFE (*quietly*) No you won't. Sit down.

HILDA What?

RAFE I said sit down.

(HILDA *is undecided.* DAISY *gives her a pleading look.*)
Pigs leave their troughs when it suits – but not civilized human beings.

WILFRED *gives* HILDA *a look of sympathetic support,* FLORENCE *gives her a reproving glance.* HAROLD *continues to eat with an air of detached interest about the outcome.* DAISY *does not want trouble, but gives* HILDA *a comforting, motherly look.*

DAISY Dad – I'll just...

RAFE *remains oddly above it all, continuing to eat naturally as he talks.* HILDA *catches* DAISY's *look and sits down, but away from the table.*

**RAFE**     No, you won't Mother. They were never spoilt when young – it 'ud be a pity to start now. One day, young woman, you may realize what words like home and family mean. A man and woman marry, they have children, feed and tend 'em, work for 'em, guide, aye, an' love 'em.

**HILDA**    Just as they ought.

**RAFE**     Aye, I agree – as they ought. Over the years they try to make a home for those children, not just a furnished place to live in, but a home, mark you, with some culture. But do those children thank you? Well, perhaps some do – mostly they don't. They take you an' your home for granted. Well, there's nobody taking me for granted.

**HILDA**    I don't see why I should eat that herring if I don't want it ...

**RAFE**     (*detached*) Then I'll tell you one reason why – as comes to mind at the moment. Pass me the bread, Florence, please. Have you ever heard of the Hunger Marchers?

             FLORENCE *passes the bread.* RAFE *takes a piece.*

**HILDA**    Yes, folk out in foreign countries.

**RAFE**     I mean folk in this country. Thank you, Florence. (*Eating as he talks.*) Something you never realized.

**WILFRED**  Must have been in the old days, Dad.

**RAFE**     It was when your brother Harold here was a babe in arms and your mother was six months carrying our Florence. That's when it was. I was out of work at the time. One day we set off to Queen's Park to have a picnic. We'd some flour cakes and a bottle of cold tea. On Chorley Old Road we suddenly came on the Hunger Marchers marching along.

**WILFRED**  Who were they, Dad, and where were they off to?

**RAFE**     They were men down from the Clydeside. Men who'd been out of work for years, and had seen their wives and families go hungry. A band of them

|          | got together to walk the four hundred miles' stretch to the Houses of Parliament. Mother, do you remember their feet, all sore and bandaged up? |
| DAISY | Yes – and I remember their faces. They were singing, weren't they? |
| RAFE | Nay, not singing, Mother, whistling. I don't think they had the strength to sing, but by heck they could whistle. |
| DAISY | Yes, they were whistling 'Loch Lomond'. |
| RAFE | (*to* HILDA) We were standing there as they went by. I can hear 'em this minute. Your mother nudged me as one weary-looking chap came up. The next thing she'd taken the flour cakes from under my arm and handed them to him. And on they went. That didn't happen in foreign countries; it happened here. And once you've lived through it you don't forget it. |
| HILDA | But it can't happen these days. |
| HAROLD | Them times are gone for ever. |
| RAFE | That's what I thought before it happened to me. |
| HAROLD | You can't have another depression – they've got economic planning that makes it impossible. |
| RAFE | If the Government suddenly decided there were too many cars on the road – and put a curb on production – there could be thousands out of work next month. |
| FLORENCE | What happened to you, Dad? |
| RAFE | (*eating as he talks*) At the mill where I'd worked from a boy they'd made me engine tenter over Nellie, as we called her. I thought I'd a job for life, looking after the engine. Till one clever official up in London decided it would pay them to close down a few hundred mills and have the machinery broken up. Economic Planning, see. |
| WILFRED | Why, Dad? |
| RAFE | Hitler were paying a big price for scrap iron, needed all he could get. It was a chance not to be missed. So they gave us all a week's notice, shut the mill down one Friday, and on the Monday after they had scrap men in, smashing the machinery up. |
| FLORENCE | Was it hard to get work in those times? |

RAFE   It wasn't all that easy – with well over half the
       country out of work, searching for jobs. It took me
       eighteen months. Hardly a week went by but they'll
       pull some poor chap out of yon canal down the
       road. (*He thumbs over his shoulder.*)

DAISY  Aye, and many a poor woman too.

WILFRED And did they smash her up – your engine, Nellie?

RAFE   What else? I told you Hitler urgently needed all the
       scrap iron he could lay hands on for making guns
       and shells and bombs. Mind you, we got most of it
       back around nineteen-forty.

HILDA  Hitler! Why bring him up? That's all a thing of the
       past – it's another world.

RAFE   It might be to you – but it's not to me.

HILDA  Well, I still don't see what all this has got to do with
       a herring.

       WILFRED *nods in agreement.* RAFE *silences him with a
       look.*

RAFE   Look at your mother – in those days she was a
       young woman, and a bonny woman, not much
       older than you are now – and she hadn't had a
       decent meal in months. She would have given
       thanks to God for that good wholesome food on
       your plate. But she was lucky to get a bit of bread
       and dripping or the odd slice of potted meat. (*With
       a rising outburst.*) So I won't have you sit there in
       front of me and see you make little of good food.
       Because you're making little of the life we've had to
       live! And millions like us.

DAISY  Dad – calm yourself.

RAFE   I can't stand the way young people are today – all
       for themselves, and all for the present, as though
       the past didn't exist.

DAISY  (*always achieving a balance of sympathy*) More tea,
       Dad?

RAFE   No, thank you, Mother – not just now. (*Rising.*) But
       there is one thing you can do for me – have that
       herring of our Hilda's safely put on one side – and
       you serve it to her, and nothing else, at every meal
       – until she eats it! I'm having no more sloppy living
       under my roof. (*He picks up his jacket.*)

HILDA    I won't eat it ...

RAFE    We'll see – because you'll eat nothing at my table until you have. (*He picks up his collar and tie.*)

HILDA    I won't touch it! Not if it's there till Kingdom come!

RAFE    Right, we'll see the outcome. I'll go and get ready for my union meeting. If you get the better of me you'll be the first in this house who has. Mother, I'm relying on you over that herring.

DAISY    I'll get it out of the way at once, Dad.

RAFE *goes out.* DAISY *has seen quarrels come and go and doesn't take them too seriously. She gives* HILDA *a pat, then goes to the kitchen with the herring.*

HAROLD    (*to* HILDA) Don't worry – they'll be comin' to take him away in the yellow cab very soon, the way he's going on. He's obsessed.

FLORENCE    (*angrily*) Don't you be so stupid!

HAROLD    What – a scene like that over a herring? He must be mad.

FLORENCE    It's not over a herring – it's over a principle. You've got to have some order in a home.

HILDA    Oh, shut up, our Florence! You're as bad as him.

WILFRED    Now then, now then, let's not row ....

FLORENCE    If she had eaten her tea there'd have been no row. She's full of likes and dislikes lately.

HAROLD    She's been on the port wine, hasn't she!

*There is a knock on the front door.*

Sumdy at door, Wilf!

FLORENCE    (*rising*) It's all right – I'll go. You know Dad detests anybody fussing over their food – not eating what's put in front of them. With half the world starving.

FLORENCE *goes out to the front door.*

HILDA    Dad – Dad – Dad – you'd think he was the only one in the house!

WILFRED    (*going to* HILDA *and putting his arms round her*) Take no notice, love.

| | |
|---|---|
| **HAROLD** | I'll lay you two-to-one you'll eat the herring. |
| **HILDA** | I will hell as like! |
| **HAROLD** | I bet you. |
| **HILDA** | You're on. |
| **HAROLD** | Right, in dollars. |
| | DAISY *enters from the kitchen.* |
| **DAISY** | Don't worry, love, I'll get you something nice later. |
| **HILDA** | I'm sorry, Mum, for causing such a rumpus. |
| **DAISY** | We'll get over it, love. |
| **HAROLD** | If you meet me at Harry Wong's new Chinese restaurant at ten-thirty after the dogs, I'll buy you a chop suey butty. |
| | *He makes a jam sandwich.* |
| | HILDA *rises and takes her handkerchief from her bag.* |
| **WILFRED** | You'll be on the borrow again if I know you – but don't come to me. |
| **HAROLD** | Don't you forget to collect my two pound. |
| | FLORENCE *enters carrying an expensively boxed parcel.* |
| **FLORENCE** | There's a parcel arrived for Dad, Mum. |
| | FLORENCE *puts the box on the table and helps* DAISY *to clear.* |
| **DAISY** | That's unusual – I wonder what it can be? |
| **WILFRED** | (*reading the label*) Horsfall and Trott, Beespoke Tailors. |
| **HAROLD** | (*rising*) Bespoke! Made to measure. I'll bet it's a fancy weskit for the engine tenters' ball. (*He does a dance step, picks up* RAFE'S *paper, and sits down.*) |
| **WILFRED** | I can't think what it can be! |
| **DAISY** | Neither can I. |
| **HAROLD** | The mysterious Mr Crompton – never lets his right hand know what his left hand is doing. |
| **WILFRED** | Listen for him coming downstairs, Mum. (*He takes out a bill.*) It's an overcoat. 'R. Crompton, Esq. One overcoat. Thirty-two guineas. Received with thanks.' |
| **HAROLD** | Thirty-three pounds twelve for an overcoat! It can't be … |
| **WILFRED** | It is! Look … |
| **HAROLD** | They must have seen him coming. |

**DAISY** If your father comes in and catches you prying into his business, I'll feel sorry for you.

**WILFRED** For thirty-two guineas from Burton's I could have got him a lovely worsted made-to-measure suit, a new spring overcoat, and have enough left over for a pair of Chelsea boots.

**HAROLD** You know what I think – as a lad he musta gone round starved to death with the cold – never knew what it was to have an overcoat – an' now he's trying to make it up to himself.

**FLORENCE** (*putting the napkins away*) You've got a bit more understanding than I thought you had.

**WILFRED** Get off – the way Dad talks of the Cromptons anybody would think they were the lords of creation.

**HAROLD** Your father's come up in the world since he had us.

**HILDA** I think it would have become him better to have paid a bit less, and bought a new coat for Mum.

**DAISY** Your dad hasn't had a new overcoat for years. (*She pushes the trolley to the kitchen.*)

**WILFRED** And I'm not expecting he'll want another. Paying that price.

**DAISY** I don't need a coat. Anyway, I could have one tomorrow if I asked him. (*She pushes the trolley inside the kitchen and returns.*)

**HILDA** You shouldn't have to ask him, Mum.

**FLORENCE** (*putting the cruet, etc., away and using the crumb-tray from the sideboard*). Will you stop causing trouble. You know Dad would give Mother anything ...

**HAROLD** If he'd a couple of gumboils he wouldn't give you one.

**HILDA** Why should he have all the say?

**DAISY** Your dad would lay down his life for me.

**HAROLD** It's not the same thing.

**DAISY** Wilf, love, hurry up, he's coming.

WILFRED *replaces the bill.* RAFE *enters. He is dressed to go to his union meeting and now wears shoes.*

**WILFRED** Dad, there's a parcel for you.

| | |
|---|---|
| **HAROLD** | It's from Horsfall and Trott's. |
| **RAFE** | (*casually*) Oh aye, then it'll be an overcoat I ordered some time back. Will you take it upstairs for me, Florence? |
| **DAISY** | But aren't you going to try it on. |
| **RAFE** | I had two fittings, so it should be all right. |
| **FLORENCE** | Go on, Dad, let's see you in it. (*She replaces the crumb-tray on the sideboard, puts the tablecloth in a drawer, and lays a runner and bowls of flowers on the table.*) |
| **DAISY** | I should think so! |
| **HAROLD** | It might not fit right, you know. (*Sotto voce.*) You can't trust these cheap tailors. |
| **WILFRED** | (*crossing to the table and taking a pair of scissors from the workbox on it*) Here you are, here's the scissors, Dad.<br>HILDA *turns away.* |
| **RAFE** | (*undoing the parcel*) Knots were made to be unfastened. It only needs patience. There we are. |
| **DAISY** | I'd like to see how it looks.<br>RAFE *pockets the bill, unfastens the string, opens the box and removes the tissue paper.* DAISY *picks up the overcoat.*<br>That's a good cloth. It is for sure. |
| **FLORENCE** | Let me, Dad. (*She rubs her face against the cloth.*) It's so soft and warm. Come on. (*She helps* RAFE *to put the coat on.*)<br>RAFE *stands centre.* WILFRED *moves to his left.* |
| **WILFRED** | Silk-lined, Dad. Hand-stitched! And look, Harold, taped seams!<br>FLORENCE *and* HILDA *pick fluff off the coat.* |
| **HAROLD** | (*aside*) Aye, one sneeze and he's naked. |
| **RAFE** | No fussing, now. Anybody'ud think you'd never seen a new topcoat. |
| **HAROLD** | (*side*) We haven't – not one as cost that much. |
| **DAISY** | (*rolling up her string*) That looks grand, Dad. |
| **WILFRED** | It's a good fit, eh, Harold? |
| **HAROLD** | Aye. (*Aside.*) It fits where it touches. |
| **RAFE** | It's none too bad for these days. |

| | |
|---|---|
| **FLORENCE** | Oh, it's lovely, Dad. You look so distinguished. |
| **RAFE** | I had a job to get the cloth. If you want the best you've got to pay for it. But it lasts that much longer. |
| | *There is a knock on the front door.* |
| **HAROLD** | Wilf, somebody at door! |
| | WILFRED *starts for the door.* HILDA *rises and looks through the window.* |
| **HILDA** | Oh, it's Arthur – shall I go, Florence? |
| **FLORENCE** | You might as well. |
| | HILDA *goes to the front door.* |
| | He told me he was working overtime. I can't think what he wants coming round here on a Friday. |
| **HAROLD** | I can't think what he wants coming round here at all. |
| **DAISY** | Show a bit more relish. He is your intended! |
| | RAFE *takes off the overcoat.* FLORENCE *folds the coat.* |
| **HILDA** | (*off*) Arthur, what a nice surprise! |
| **ARTHUR** | (*off*) Hello, Hilda. |
| | ARTHUR *enters with* HILDA. *He is a sheet metal worker, a quiet likeable chap of thirty, wearing overalls. He and* FLORENCE *look at each other.* HILDA *moves to the sofa and sits.* WILFRED *stands by the piano.* |
| | Oh, hullo, Mr Crompton. |
| **RAFE** | Good evening, Arthur. |
| **DAISY** | Well, how nice to see you, Arthur. |
| **HAROLD** WILFRED | } (*together*) Howgo, Arthur. |
| **ARTHUR** | Hullo, Mother. I'm sorry to butt in like this ... |
| **RAFE** | (*moving to the desk*) Never be ashamed of a bit of honest dirt, lad; there's not enough of it knocking about these days. |
| | (*He glances at* HAROLD.) Will you put the coat upstairs for me, Mother? |
| **FLORENCE** | Let me, Dad. It's all right, Mother. |
| **RAFE** | Thanks. Put it at the back – I'll not be needing it for some time. |

| FLORENCE | (*to* ARTHUR) I thought you said you'd be working overtime. |
|---|---|
| **ARTHUR** | I am. I've got to go back. |
| **FLORENCE** | Nothing wrong, is there? |
| **ARTHUR** | No, I've just come round to ask you something. |
| **FLORENCE** | I expect it'll keep a minute or two. Oh, Dad, I'll put that cover on it to protect it. (*To* ARTHUR, *as she passes.*) My dad's new overcoat. Just look at it. I wish you had one like it. |

FLORENCE *goes out.*

| **ARTHUR** | That looks a gradely bit of topcoating, Mr Crompton. |
| **RAFE** | (*reading a letter at the desk*) Always buy the best – if you can afford it – you won't go far wrong. I detest anything cheap or shoddy. |
| **HAROLD** | I'll bet it didn't cost much under fifteen quid, Dad! |
| **RAFE** | It cost thirty-two guineas. |

DAISY *gives* HAROLD *a look and goes out to the kitchen with the box.*

| **HAROLD** | Thirty-two guineas! Cash down! Why, for that I could have bought you a ... |
| **RAFE** | (*cutting in*) You couldn't have bought me a better coat. My suit upstairs cost me twenty-one guineas. I've had it twelve year and it's like new! |
| **HAROLD** | If you have it another nine it'll work out a guinea a year. |

DAISY *enters from the kitchen.*

| **RAFE** | So it will. Remember that Welsh flannel shirt I had, Mother – must have worn it about five years regular, and it's still good. (*He puts the letter and bill in the desk, and takes out his union book.*) |
| **DAISY** | It used to be a heck of a job washing it. Is everything all right with you, Arthur? |
| **ARTHUR** | I'll tell you better when I've had a word with your Florence. |
| **DAISY** | You mustn't mind if she's a bit short with you, Arthur. It's just her way. |

| | |
|---|---|
| **ARTHUR** | Oh, I know that. I've grown used to it by this. |
| **DAISY** | She's a real good lass at heart. |
| **ARTHUR** | Aye, I know that too. Or else I wouldn't be here. |
| **DAISY** | Have you had something to eat? |
| **ARTHUR** | Yes, thank you, Mother. I've had my tea – gammon rashers. |

*The others react.* RAFE *makes notes from his union book.*

| | |
|---|---|
| **DAISY** | Well, I expect you could do with another cup of tea. |
| **ARTHUR** | Now, don't go to any bother. |
| **DAISY** | It's no bother, Arthur. |
| **ARTHUR** | Thanks, I do feel a bit dry. |
| **HAROLD** | Aye, they're inclined to be salty. |

DAISY *goes to the kitchen, switching on the light.*

| | |
|---|---|
| **HILDA** | (*rising and offering a chair*) Come and sit down here, Arthur, and make yourself at home. You can't be in such a hurry. |
| **ARTHUR** | Thanks, Hilda. (*He puts his cap in his pocket, and sits.*) |
| **HILDA** | You look a bit tired. |
| **ARTHUR** | So do you. I mean not as chirpy as usual. |

HILDA *returns to her seat.* HAROLD *and* WILFRED *gaze at* ARTHUR. *There is an uncomfortable pause.*

| | |
|---|---|
| **WILFRED** | How are things in general, Arthur? |
| **ARTHUR** | Oh – er – fair to middlin'. |

WILFRED *and* HAROLD *nod, smiling.*

| | |
|---|---|
| **WILFRED** | I see they keep you at it. |
| **ARTHUR** | Yes, yes, we keep on the go. |

*Everyone nods enthusiastically.*

| | |
|---|---|
| **HAROLD** | Old Aspinall always has plenty of jobs lined up outside. |
| **ARTHUR** | Yes, it's our busy time, just before the Easter holiday. But we're nearly straight. (*He takes out a cigarette packet.*) |

*The others watch in stunned silence as* ARTHUR *taps the cigarette, puts it in his mouth and feels in his pocket for his lighter.* RAFE *turns.* ARTHUR *quickly replaces the cigarette.* FLORENCE *enters.*

| | |
|---|---|
| **FLORENCE** | Well now, what brought you round? |
| | ARTHUR *rises and gives* FLORENCE *his seat.* |
| **ARTHUR** | I've got some news about old Aspinall. |
| **RAFE** | Don't say he's retiring at last! |
| **ARTHUR** | How did you guess? He's bought a bungalow at Lytham-St-Annes. |
| **RAFE** | He could have bought Lytham-St-Annes itself, the money he's been making out of that tinkering business. |
| **WILFRED** | You mean sheet-metal works, Dad. |
| **RAFE** | He started out as a tinker and in my eyes a tinker he'll always be. |
| **ARTHUR** | You can set out as one thing – but end up as another. |
| **RAFE** | I suppose so – except he's got a tinker mentality. It was in his family. |
| **ARTHUR** | I don't care what he has, Mr Crompton – but I will guarantee any job I put my hand to. Any job at all. |
| **HAROLD** | There's not many British workmen can say that nowadays, eh, Dad? |
| **RAFE** | (*locking the desk*) No – not whose word I'd take. |
| **FLORENCE** | Is he talking of selling up or something? |
| **ARTHUR** | (*sitting*) Oh, no, he wouldn't sell out. He'll always want a finger in the pie. |
| | DAISY *enters from the kitchen with a cup of tea and a piece of cake which she hands to* ARTHUR. |
| **DAISY** | Here y'are, Arthur, love. Are you sure you wouldn't like something cooked? |
| **HAROLD** | Happen a nice fried herring. |
| | *There is a disapproving reaction from the others.* |
| **ARTHUR** | This'll be fine, thanks. I'm not all that partial to fish. |
| | DAISY *crosses to the kitchen, switches off the light, takes her workbasket and sits in the armchair to darn a sock.* |
| **FLORENCE** | If he's not selling up – what is he thinking of doing? |
| **DAISY** | Give Arthur time to tell you. |
| **FLORENCE** | It's taking him long enough. |
| **ARTHUR** | They're going to move to Lytham. |

| | |
|---|---|
| **FLORENCE** | Where do you come into it? |
| **ARTHUR** | Well, in a way, that was what I came to see you about. |
| | *He looks uneasy and rises, putting his cap and plate on the table.* |
| | Shall we ... can we have a word in private? |
| **RAFE** | Speak up, Arthur. We don't hide anything in this house. |
| **FLORENCE** | Yes, out with it! |
| **ARTHUR** | Well, he came round to my bench this afternoon, and he said to me, 'I'm on the lookout for somebody as could fill the job of a proper working manager, Arthur, and I need him at once. I've got to have a chap that can estimate jobs and handle the men,' he said. 'But he must be a man as isn't in a hurry to get home of a night. In short, a married man.' |
| **FLORENCE** | Oh – I see. |
| **RAFE** | What has he got behind his mind? |
| **ARTHUR** | Then he said he'd be willing to put me in charge, if me and your Florence would get wed – soon like. Tie the whole thing up, you see. |
| **RAFE** | Aye, but suppose she doesn't want to get married in a rush? |
| **DAISY** | It's not as though they're strangers – they've been engaged a year. |
| **RAFE** | What's a year in a lifetime? |
| **WILFRED** | You grab him, Flo, while you've got the chance. |
| **RAFE** | When we need your advice we'll ask you. Who does Alf Aspinall think he is – dictating to folk just when they should get married? |
| **FLORENCE** | Yes, just because he's found the right bungalow at Lytham. We've not enough money saved up, have we? Not for such a rush. |
| **DAISY** | There's times when you've got to take a chance. |
| **RAFE** | There's enough chances to marriage without taking any extra ones. |
| **HAROLD** | It's an offer not to be sneezed at. |
| **RAFE** | Nobody's sneezing. And I'll thank you not to dip your nib where there's no ink. |

| | |
|---|---|
| **DAISY** | (*rising and fetching* RAFE'S *old overcoat, cap and scarf from the hall*) I must say it doesn't seem at all unreasonable to me, Arthur. |
| **ARTHUR** | No, it's just that he'd be more content with a married man in charge. |
| **RAFE** | 'Course he would. You've got a better hold on a man once he's married. A wife, children – all hostages to fortune. |
| | DAISY *helps* RAFE *on with his overcoat.* |
| **ARTHUR** | I don't think he wants a hold on me. He'd just like to get settled. |
| **RAFE** | Look, Arthur, I don't mind what he asks you, or tells you to do. (*He attempts to put his hand in his sleeve, but stops to gesture.*) But what does he imagine I am – that I'd let one of my daughters marry at the bidding of a tinker? |
| **ARTHUR** | I don't know what he imagines you are, Mr Crompton. |
| **RAFE** | You take things lying down in this life, and every upstart will trample over you. (*He gets his coat on.*) |
| **FLORENCE** | What do you think? What extra would you get out of it? |
| **ARTHUR** | (*Sitting again*) I think it'd be a fifty bob a week rise. A staff job, see – paid work or play. |
| **RAFE** | Aye, but not for overtime. |
| **DAISY** | You can't have everything. |
| **ARTHUR** | There'd be no broken weeks for illness or nowt like that. And I might get him to meet me half-way on overtime. |
| **RAFE** | You wouldn't want our Florence to go on teaching once she were married. |
| **ARTHUR** | If know your Florence she'll do as she thinks fit. Not what I want. |
| **WILFRED** | It's up to you to put your foot down. |
| **HAROLD** | Why shouldn't she teach? The government is going mad for married teachers. |
| **RAFE** | I'd certainly never let a wife of mine go out to work. |
| **HAROLD** | (*aside*) She wouldn't have time. |

RAFE *slowly turns to* HAROLD. DAISY *intercepts him, handing him his scarf.*

RAFE  If I couldn't keep a wife I wouldn't get wed.

DAISY  Things have changed, Dad. There's no shame to it in these times. (*She hands* RAFE *his cap, then returns to her seat and darns.*)

WILFRED  'Course, if they had youngsters soon she couldn't.

RAFE  What's that?

HAROLD  He said if they had youngsters soon she couldn't.

FLORENCE  (*rising*) Give us time to get married.

WILFRED  Oh, I meant inside matrimony.

HAROLD  (*hitting* WILFRED *with his paper*) Shut up, Wilf.

DAISY  Two-pounds-ten a week is a very good rise.

RAFE  Aye, but no overtime pay.

ARTHUR  It's not just the rise, you know. There'd be that gable-end house to go with it.

FLORENCE  It's not quite what I had in mind.

DAISY  But it's a marvellous start in these days, love. What some folk wouldn't give for that!

ARTHUR  He had a new bath put in about a year ago, and beautified throughout. A give-away rent, and no travelling.

HAROLD  Aye, houses aren't easy to come by.

ARTHUR  And a free telephone

RAFE  That house simply means that you and our Florence would act as unpaid watchmen for Mr Alf Aspinall's premises. He's got you there, living on the job. Folk knocking day and night. And keep answering the free telephone.

ARTHUR  I like my job. I'm not a clock watcher. I don't mind doing a bit extra. And it struck me we might buy ourselves a caravan near the coast – and we could get away at week-ends. You can't have it all ways. (*He looks from* FLORENCE *to* RAFE, *but gets nothing.*)

RAFE  That's your side of the matter, Arthur. And there's a lot to be said for it, I admit. But what I wouldn't stand for is the way he's going about it. Does he

|  |  |
|---|---|
| | think I've brought my daughter up all these years, then he'll decide just when she'll get married? He must think we're living in feudal times. |
| **ARTHUR** | I don't know what he thinks, Mr Crompton. I'm all mithered. |
| **RAFE** | Aye, I would be, in your shoes. I know what I'd say to any boss who tried to tell me when I should get married! He wouldn't tell me twice! |
| **ARTHUR** | He didn't actually tell me. |
| **RAFE** | That's even worse – he's trying to wheedle you into it. |
| **ARTHUR** | It all sounds different now – the way you put it, Mr Crompton. |
| **DAISY** | (*rising and moving to the door*) Now, don't get yourself late for union, Dad. |
| **RAFE** | Eh? Oh – don't worry about that, Mother. If there's not a full quorum I'll break up the meeting. (*He puts his union book in his pocket and moves to the door.*) |
| **WILFRED** | Not again, Dad! |
| **RAFE** | I believe in sticking by the rules. They were put there for a purpose. An' yon new secretary is getting a bit high-handed. They're all the same once they get in office. (*Moving down stage.*) Same as I say, about marriage – there's nothing to just getting wed. They'll do you at any registry office for twelve-and-six. |
| **HAROLD** | Seventeen-and-six. It's gone up. |
| **RAFE** | Seventeen-and-six then – but to make a decent home in life – one in which a family can grow – that needs careful preparation. If you're the lass I think you are, Florence, you'll tell Mr Alf Aspinall when a Crompton gets married they choose the time – not him! |
| **HAROLD** | I can't see what you have to worry about! |
| **RAFE** | Eh? That's my business. Let's say I don't want a slight from a tinker. No offence to you, Arthur. You're only doing the errand you've been sent on. Good night, Mother. Good night, everybody. |
| **FLORENCE** | Good night, Dad. |

| | |
|---|---|
| **WILFRED** | Ta ra, Dad. |
| | DAISY *and* RAFE *go out.* |
| **DAISY** | (*off*) Go careful now, Dad. |
| | RAFE *is heard going through the front door,* DAISY *seeing him to the gate.* |
| **HILDA** | Good night and good shuttance! |
| | HAROLD *rises and hands out cigarettes to* ARTHUR *and Wilfred.* |
| **HAROLD** | What a pity families have to have fathers! Cigarette, Arthur? Homes would be so much happier without 'em. |
| **HILDA** | This one would – that's for sure. |
| **FLORENCE** | You'd notice it if he were gone. |
| | ARTHUR *and* WILFRED *light their cigarettes.* |
| **HAROLD** | Aye, I noticed when that boil went from the back of my neck – but I'm a damn sight happier without it. |
| **ARTHUR** | I don't think you handle him right. You should tell him straight to his face. |
| **WILFRED** | See what happened to you when you did that! |
| **ARTHUR** | I feel I put my case very badly. |
| **HAROLD** | He took it very badly. |
| **HILDA** | (*rising to above the table*) Our Florence, I think you must be out of your mind turning Arthur down like that. |
| **WILFRED** | So do I! |
| **FLORENCE** | Who says I'm turning him down? Don't jump to conclusions. |
| **HILDA** | You didn't sound all that keen. |
| **FLORENCE** | (*plumping the cushions on the sofa*) I've got to think it over, haven't I? I don't believe in rushing things. |
| **ARTHUR** | Well, I admit it's sudden – in one way. |
| **HILDA** | (*moving to left of* ARTHUR) You wouldn't have to ask me twice, Arthur. |
| **WILFRED** | Me neither. |
| **HAROLD** | (*looking* WILFRED *up and down*) Wilfred! |
| **WILFRED** | I mean if I were a woman. |
| **HAROLD** | (*smiling*) The bride was given away by that well-known plastic surgeon … |

| | |
|---|---|
| **WILFRED** | Oh shut up! I only meant ... |

DAISY *enters.* HAROLD *sits on the edge of the table.*
WILFRED *stands at the piano.*

| | |
|---|---|
| **HILDA** | Mum, what have you done with that bloody herring? |
| **FLORENCE** | Hilda! |

FLORENCE *and* ARTHUR *sit on the sofa and talk
together,* FLORENCE *up stage.*

| | |
|---|---|
| **DAISY** | What for, love? |
| **HAROLD** | She's come over peckish. |
| **HILDA** | Peckish? I'll fling the rotten thing behind the fire! |
| **HAROLD** | You wouldn't dare. |
| **HILDA** | Who wouldn't! I'll show you. |
| **WILFRED** | Now then, love, you'll only get my mum into trouble. |
| **DAISY** | Ee, I don't mind, love. I'm used to it. I'll go and make you a nice egg and bacon sandwich. |
| **HILDA** | I don't think I could eat one. |
| **DAISY** | You'll feel better when you've had something to eat. Excuse me, Arthur. |

DAISY *goes out to the kitchen.*

| | |
|---|---|
| **HAROLD** | Now suppose there's not a full quorum and he comes back and catches you scoffing double deckers? |
| **HILDA** | I tell you I don't care a tinker's cuss for him. Pardon the expression, Arthur. |
| **ARTHUR** | (*half rising*) Don't mind me! |
| **WILFRED** | Arthur's a welder – not a tinker. |
| **HAROLD** | She doesn't care a welder's cuss! |
| **HILDA** | And I'm the only one in the family who doesn't care for him. |
| **HAROLD** | I'm not worrying about you. It's old Daisy – she's the one who has to carry the can back when owt goes wrong. She's going humpbacked as it is with worry. |
| **WILFRED** | Aye, poor old Mum is the one who catches out in the end. |
| **HILDA** | Oh, blast him! Sorry, Arthur, for going off – you must think we're a right funny lot. |

| | |
|---|---|
| ARTHUR | Not particularly. (*He puts his cigarette out on his shoe.*) |
| WILFRED | Thanks, Arthur. |
| FLORENCE | It's just our Hilda – I think she must be having a bout of growing pains. |
| HILDA | Oh, am I – then it's high time you had a bout of 'em too! Perhaps you wouldn't be as bloomin' stuffy as you are. |
| | ARTHUR *reacts.* |
| HAROLD | Don't worry, Arthur. I think she's got a touch of the spring. |
| FLORENCE | And she's been on port wine. |
| HAROLD | Oh, aye – spring an' port wine – enough to go to any girl's head. (*He flicks* HILDA'S *hair.*) |
| HILDA | (*rising and facing* ARTHUR) I'll tell you what it is, Arthur, it's our rotten old father ... |
| WILFRED | Hilda, love ... |
| FLORENCE | (*rising*) Hilda – what a thing to come out with! |
| HILDA | (*moving up stage*) I'm not ashamed to tell it – it's Mr Bighead Crompton who insists I've got to eat a bloomin' cold stinking herring that's out there on the kitchen shelf. |
| FLORENCE | (*moving to the head of the table*) Our Hilda – don't talk like that! |
| HILDA | Oh, dry up! If you heard the girls in the mill going on you'd realize how behind the times we are. Why, Betty Partington is off to an all-night rave up tonight! |
| FLORENCE | When I hear you talk of the times I'm glad I'm behind them. |
| WILFRED | Aye, but don't hold others back. |
| HAROLD | (*rising*) All-night twist party! What about it, Arthur? Fancy your chances? There'll be plenty of young stuff there. |
| ARTHUR | (*half rising*) Aye, I wouldn't mind... |
| FLORENCE | You'll stay where you are. (*to* HILDA.) Is that what you want – all-night parties? |
| HILDA | She won't get home till tomorrow diner-time – yet nothing will be said. I'd like to see his face if I suggested it. |
| FLORENCE | Yes, because your father cares for you. |

| | |
|---|---|
| **HILDA** | He cares for his bloomin' self… |
| **WILFRED** | No – I think he honestly cares. |
| **HILDA** | Then he's a funny way of showing it. |
| **FLORENCE** | (*sitting on the sofa*) I'm sorry about her, Arthur. How's your mother keeping? |
| **ARTHUR** | It's all right. I understand how your Hilda feels. My mother's all right except when her back's plaguing her. |
| **HAROLD** | (*to* FLORENCE) Now you know. |
| **HILDA** | (*to* FLORENCE) It's your own father you should feel ashamed of – not me. What do you say, Harold? |
| **HAROLD** | (*moving to the table and sitting astride a chair*) Arthur, do you know in this day and age we're expected to hand over to him the best part of our wages every Friday? To him! |
| **FLORENCE** | (*rising*) Do you lot want keeping for nothing? It's same as my dad says – it's not a lodging house – it's a home – and a good one too. |
| **WILFRED** | Even a bad home is better than none at all. |
| **FLORENCE** | You try and find digs as good as your own home – you'll see what they'll charge you in these days! WILFRED *wanders down stage.* |
| **HAROLD** | I've a good mind to! I have – honest. |
| **ARTHUR** | I think I would if I were you, Harold. I'd go out and get myself a room somewhere. |
| **HAROLD** | Aye, I would, only I don't fancy living on my own in a furnished room – listening to my own jokes like. |
| **WILFRED** | I can't say I blame you. |
| **ARTHUR** | If you don't think handing over is right, Harold, you tell him. I would. |
| **FLORENCE** | (*to* ARTHUR) Don't be so liberal with your advice. You're not a member of the family yet! (*She moves above the table.*) |
| **HILDA** | (*to* ARTHUR) God help you on that day! (*To* HAROLD.) Yes – you great soft ha'porth – if you'd had enough guts you'd have stood up to him before this. |
| **WILFRED** | 'Course he would! |

**FLORENCE**  Why – what has our Harold to stand up for? Eh? Greyhounds tonight – Wanderers tomorrow afternoon – boozing tomorrow night and Sunday the strip club.

**HAROLD**  (*unabashed*) Every man to his taste. I'm doing nobody any harm.

**FLORENCE**  Have you never thought of doing some good, for a change?

**HAROLD**  Not when I look at him and see where it gets you. Besides, think of the fun I get going my way and spiting him.

**ARTHUR**  A man's only as big as you let him be. I'd stand up to him.

**FLORENCE**  Would you? I very much doubt it.

**HAROLD**  So do I – come to that.

**HILDA**  (*rising; to* FLORENCE) You think there's no-one like him!

**HAROLD**  There isn't, thank God. Oh, but come Sunday tea-time and he gets one of his old-time moods on him, I'll bet you'll be standing there by the piano singing Handel with him!

**WILFRED**  Aye, I wouldn't be surprised. He can be very persuasive.

**HILDA**  Me! If ever I sing with that one again I hope the first note chokes me.

*She moves up to the piano.*

**ARTHUR**  Hilda, love ...!

**WILFRED**  Don't talk like that, love. It's not like you.

**FLORENCE**  (*to* ARTHUR) I don't know what's come over our Hilda lately.

**HAROLD**  It's all come about since her Donald threw her over.

**HILDA**  I threw him over – if you want to know.

**HAROLD**  (*singing to the tune of 'Allan Water'*)
For his bride
A soldier sought her,

**WILFRED**  You mean a flight sergeant.

**HAROLD**  But a sergeant false was he,
On the banks of Allan Water,
None so fair as she.
On the banks ...

WILFRED *gestures to* HAROLD *to be quiet.*

**HILDA** (*shouting*) Stop it! (*She runs to* HAROLD *and shakes his shoulder.*) Stop it! Leave me alone. (*She runs away, sits on the pouffe and sobs.*)

DAISY *enters from the kitchen and goes to pick up the cup and plate.*

**DAISY** Hilda, love, your tea's nearly ready. Ee, what's come over you, child?

**ARTHUR** (*crossing to* HILDA *and putting his hands on her shoulders*) Now then, Hilda love, don't let yourself get upset like that.

**HILDA** (*sobbing*) Sorry, Arthur. (*She puts her hand on his.*)

**ARTHUR** Have your cry out, love, and then go and have your tea. You'll feel fine then.

**HILDA** I wish you'd come and asked me to marry you, Arthur. I'd be packed and out of that door with you by this.

**WILFRED** But he hasn't. So have your tea instead.

**HAROLD** I'm sorry I upset you about Donald, love. It might not be too late – if she turns him down you can move in ... Blimey! (*Rising.*) I've nearly missed the first race. See you, Arthur.

HAROLD *takes his cap from the piano and goes out to the kitchen.*

**DAISY** Wilf, it's nearly seven.

**WILFRED** What? Oh, Betsy Jane! I'd better go and stake my claim.

WILFRED *goes out to the kitchen and puts his cigarette out.*

**DAISY** Better not leave it too late. Hilda, we mustn't let your bacon burn.

**HILDA** (*rising*) No, we mustn't.

HAROLD *enters the scullery and rubs his shoes.*

**ARTHUR** (*moving up stage, taking his cap from his pocket*) Ee, I'd better be off, too. I'll have to make a dash for it.

**DAISY** Didn't you come to ask our Florence something?

**ARTHUR** Did I? Yes, I suppose I did.

**DAISY** (*taking* ARTHUR'S *cap and putting it on the piano stool*) Then don't go without your answer. Come on, Hilda, we don't want to be in the way.

DAISY *and* HILDA *go out to the kitchen.* WILFRED *enters the scullery.*

**HAROLD**  (*putting on his scarf and cap*) I'll lay you two to one she turns him down.

FLORENCE *fetches her briefcase, sits at the head of the table, puts on her spectacles, and starts to mark exercise books.*

**WILFRED**  Who?

**HAROLD**  Our Florence, you nit, turns Arthur down. And I'll give you even money our Hilda nips in and takes her place.

**WILFRED**  If Florence doesn't marry Arthur she'll marry nobody.

**HAROLD**  Your sister Flo is father-fixated. If I know anything, she'll be living here, looking after her dad, when he's bloody ninety.

**WILFRED**  Aye, and if I know anything, the way you're going on, you'll be keeping 'em company!

WILFRED *and* HAROLD *go out through the back door.*

**ARTHUR**  Well, Florence, what shall I tell old Aspinall?

**FLORENCE**  I'm not sure. It's same as Dad says – you don't want to go rushing blindly into marriage.

**ARTHUR**  We're not all that blind, are we? I say, don't you think he's taking things a bit far with your Hilda ...?

**FLORENCE**  Don't mention that kipper again to me!

**ARTHUR**  Stomachs are very funny things.

**FLORENCE**  Only when they get out of hand.

**ARTHUR**  Have you noticed anything different about your Hilda lately?

**FLORENCE**  Such as what?

**ARTHUR**  I don't know. It was just a feeling I got. She seems older in some way, different like.

**FLORENCE**  I'll tell you what I did notice. I noticed how you took her in your arms.

**ARTHUR**  You mean when she was crying? You didn't mind that, did you?

**FLORENCE**  No – I didn't mind – except the thought struck me at that moment – you never take me in your arms like that – do you?

**ARTHUR** Well, you never cry. I've to see the first time yet.

**FLORENCE** That doesn't mean to say there aren't times when I could cry.

**ARTHUR** I know you hold yourself in a lot. It's not always for the best.

**FLORENCE** I can only be as I am. You're very fond of our Hilda, aren't you?

**ARTHUR** Yes, I suppose I am. Why?

**FLORENCE** Perhaps you're more fond of her than you are of me?

**ARTHUR** Aye, it could be, could be.

**FLORENCE** Happen you've got engaged to the wrong one?

**ARTHUR** Aye, I might have. You never know.

**FLORENCE** Oh! I see. Thanks for being honest.

**ARTHUR** Not at all. But there is one little difference. When I go off to work now, I shan't be thinking of your Hilda, I'll be thinking of you. When I close my eyes at night, I don't see your Hilda, I see you. I am very fond of your Hilda, but I love you, and I can't live without you.

**FLORENCE** Oh, Arthur! (*She takes off her glasses and looks at him.*)

**ARTHUR** And I don't care a damn about the job – the house – old Aspinall – or, come to that, your domineering, know-all father!

FLORENCE *is unexpectedly touched, and rises.* ARTHUR *and* FLORENCE *approach each other and embrace passionately.* HILDA *enters from the kitchen just taking a big bite at a sandwich. She stops dead, her mouth full, and stares at the pair, unseen by them, then starts to back stealthily into the kitchen. The door opens and* RAFE *enters.*

**RAFE** Mother – I'm back. There wasn't a full ... (*He spots the couple and stops.*)

FLORENCE *tries to break away from the embrace and looks from* ARTHUR *to* RAFE. DAISY *enters from the kitchen.*

**DAISY**  Ee – Dad – so you broke up the ...

DAISY *breaks off when she sees* RAFE *staring at* ARTHUR *and* FLORENCE. *Then it strikes her that she had better push* HILDA *out of sight, which she does, as* RAFE *looks across and —*

*The* CURTAIN *falls*

# ACT TWO

*The same. Sunday, tea-time.*

*The home has a Sunday look. There are flowers in vases and the
table is laid for high tea, with the best cloth and the best china.*

*When the curtain rises, church bells are ringing.* WILFRED,
*wearing a white shirt, tie and pullover, is reading the 'News of
the World'.* DAISY *enters from the kitchen wearing a nice frock
and Dutch apron, and carrying a large cake which she puts on
the table.*

| | |
|---|---|
| **WILFRED** | Hy, Mum! |
| **DAISY** | Yes, love? |
| **WILFRED** | Did Betsy Jane come in like she said? |
| **DAISY** | You mean with the five pounds? |
| **WILFRED** | Yes. |
| **DAISY** | I'm afraid not, but she promised me she'd let us have it back for certain tomorrow morning. |
| **WILFRED** | I can't wait till then. It means I won't see it till tomorrow night. I'm all but skint. |
| | DAISY *goes to her handbag on the sideboard and gets out three pound notes.* |
| **DAISY** | (*crossing to* WILFRED) Here you are, love, your three pounds. |
| **WILFRED** | What? Oh, no, Mum, I can't take it! It'll only get you in a mess. |
| **DAISY** | Go on – I let you in for it. |
| **WILFRED** | (*taking the notes*) Ta. Very good of you. I don't know how you do it. |
| **DAISY** | Neither do I. |
| **WILFRED** | How will she get it? |

47

DAISY    I don't care how she gets it so long as she hands me
         my five pounds back. I've had a very dodgy
         weekend, one way and another.

WILFRED  Aye – and it's not over yet! I say, Mum, surely my
         dad won't have our Hilda's herring stuck in front of
         her at Sunday tea table?

DAISY    You know your dad – once he sets his mind on
         something, it takes a bit of shifting.

WILFRED  You kidding! When I saw you fetch that thing out at
         dinner–time I coulda dropped with the shock. There
         we all were with our plates of roast beef and
         Yorkshire!

DAISY    (*sitting*) She'll not starve while I'm around.

WILFRED  You've gotta hand it to him – when he says
         something he means it. But what is it makes him go
         like that, Mum, blind to everything except what he
         has his mind on?

DAISY    He's always been the same – he's got to work things
         out of his system.

WILFRED  Then he should take a dose of Epsom salts. Besides,
         it's getting a bit high.

DAISY    I agree it's not a nice thing to put in front of
         somebody.

WILFRED  (*rising*) It's a bloody shame. That's what it is. Is
         there nothing you can do?

DAISY    It'll have to sort itself out.

WILFRED  It'll never sort itself out. Summat's got to be done.

DAISY    Don't let your dad catch you with the *News of the
         World*.

         HILDA *enters*.

WILFRED  I don't care what the hell he catches me with. I've
         stood about enough of that fellow. Hello, Hilda.

HILDA    Hello, Wilf.

         WILFRED *goes out to the kitchen*.

         What's up with our Wilf, Mum?

DAISY    Have a nice rest, love?

HILDA    I had a good read and a good think.

DAISY    He's worried about you.

HILDA    I wish he wouldn't take on so for me.
         WILFRED *enters the scullery and goes out through the*
         *back door.*

DAISY    He always has done (*Rising.*) Hold on a tick. I've
         got you something nice.
         DAISY *goes to the kitchen.*

HILDA    (*calling*) I noticed it at dinner-time. He hardly
         touched his meat. (*Her eyes fall on a book of poetry*
         *on* RAFE'S *chair. She picks it up and opens it.*)
         DAISY *enters with a plate covered with a napkin.*

DAISY    Beef sandwiches. I did 'em on the sly. Get 'em
         down you afore he gets back.

HILDA    Where's he gone?

DAISY    Taking his Sunday constitutional round the moors.
         Remember the time when he used to insist on
         taking us all with him – oh, my poor legs. (*She*
         *pushes the plate at* HILDA.)

HILDA    (*putting the poetry book on the piano*) No, thanks,
         Mum – I won't have anything to eat.

DAISY    You won't? Why not? Aren't you hungry?

HILDA    I've made a resolution.

DAISY    What about?

HILDA    I'm resolved to eat that flamin' herring, Mum!

DAISY    Ee, you're not, are you? You mean you're going to
         give way?

HILDA    I feel I can't stand it much longer. All the tension
         like. It's not just for myself – I'd starve to death
         sooner than give in – it's what it does to the home.

DAISY    Aye, there's something about your dad as can drive
         you that way – round the bend, as they say. Yet he
         means well, bless him.

HILDA    Have you felt it, Mum?

DAISY    Felt it! Ee, child, there's been times when I've felt so
         pulled out of myself, among the lot of you, that I've
         wished I could go and live amongst strangers for a
         week or two, just to get my bearings again. But a
         mother has to keep these feelings to herself.

**HILDA**  Whenever there's trouble you've always had to act as buffer between him and us.

**DAISY**  That's what I'm here for.

**HILDA**  Life's not been easy for you, Mum, with him.

**DAISY**  I've had my happy times, love. And I've brought a lot of the rest of it on myself. Here, shall I tell you something – you'll no sooner put your fork into that herring than he'll up and say: 'It's all right, Hilda. Don't eat it! Don't touch it' I know him. He can't stand being bested. Then he's sorry once he's bested you.

*HAROLD passes the window to the front door.*

**HILDA**  Ah, but that's where I catch him! I don't care what he says – once I start I'll not give way. I'll devour every tiny morsel of that bloomin' herring – yes – skin, tail, fins – the lot – even if it makes me sick! I'll put him through it.

**DAISY**  Peace in the home at last.

*HAROLD enters. DAISY and HILDA are startled and try to hide the sandwiches. The light starts to fade slowly as dusk falls.*

**HAROLD**  Aye-aye! Now what're you two scheming up?

**DAISY**  You gave me a shock.

**HILDA**  Yes, I thought it was him.

**HAROLD**  Who – old droopy-drawers? He'll be in shortly. I saw him stepping it out, and I spotted Arthur and our Florence hanging well behind, keeping out of his reach.

**HILDA**  I can't say I blame them.

**DAISY**  Poor Dad, always on his own.

**HAROLD**  You get as you prefer his room to his company. Mum, did you *have* to marry him?

**DAISY**  How dare you!

**HILDA**  Our Harold!

**HAROLD**  No, I didn't mean it like that. I mean could you not find yourself somebody better?

**DAISY**  He was a handsome young man in those days, was your dad. He'd make two of you.

**HAROLD**  Gaa – him!

HILDA    Talking about marriage – have our Florence and
         Arthur decided on it?

DAISY    Not as I know of for sure. But I thought our
         Florence was looking different ...

HAROLD   The same thought struck me – sort of hopeful like.
         She was clutching on to Arthur's arm.

HILDA    She's got to make up her mind between him and
         my dad. (*Moving to the kitchen.*) I'll get these out of
         the way.

HAROLD   Oh, it's like that, is it? Just fancy!
         HILDA *goes to the kitchen with the sandwiches.*
         Hy, Mum, has old Guinness-guts handed over yet?

DAISY    Betsy-Jane? No, but she will for certain in the
         morning.

HAROLD   I'll have a job to wait. I've run out of fags as it is.
         DAISY *rises and goes to her handbag.*

DAISY    Here you are, love, your two pounds.

HAROLD   No, Mum, I can't take it.

DAISY    Here you are – it was on my behalf.

HAROLD   Ta. Now, are you sure you can spare it?

DAISY    No – I can't. But I'll have to.

HAROLD   I'm not codding – you can have it back.

DAISY    I'll just about manage till tomorrow morning. But
         I'm beginning to see there's a lot in what your dad
         says – 'neither a borrower nor a lender be'.

HAROLD   Aye, except the loss of the friend in Betsy Jane's
         case would be a positive advantage.
         RAFE *approaches the front door.*
         Blimey, here he is – I'll be off.
         HAROLD *goes to the kitchen.* RAFE *enters the front door.*
         DAISY *opens the living room door for him.* RAFE *hangs
         his cap up on the hallstand. He is wearing a tweedy
         suit and cap, and carries a sprig of white heather.*

DAISY    Hello, Dad. You're back in time for tea.

RAFE     (*entering the room*) Good. I'm ready for it. (*Looking
         round.*) Is our Hilda in?

DAISY    Yes. She's in the kitchen.

RAFE   Look what I found you on the moors – a sprig of white heather.

DAISY  Oh, how nice! Let's hope it brings me luck. (*She kisses* RAFE.)

RAFE   I've had time to think things over and I fancy the lesson has gone home.

DAISY  (*closing the door and putting the heather in her buttonhole*) What lesson? Oh, you mean with our Hilda and the herring.

RAFE   (*sitting in his armchair*) Aye. It was a bit of a challenge, see, and I wasn't going to back down. But it's served its purpose. And d'you know, I couldn't say I've enjoyed a meal since it started. At our age we can't stand up to tension same as the young 'uns.

DAISY  So you don't want me to bother with the herring any more?

RAFE   Eh? But of course you must bring the herring in. She musn't get the idea in her head she's bested me.

DAISY  What then? What do you want? I'm getting at my wits' end.

RAFE   If you are, don't let them see it – they don't think we're supposed to have any human weaknesses. You fetch the herring in, see, and put it in front of her. Now if she so much as touches her knife and fork, I'll whip that herring away. To be honest with you I'm fed up with the sight of the damn thing myself.

DAISY  No more than I am!

RAFE   You know, I never really intended her to have to eat it.

DAISY  Well, she wasn't to know that.

RAFE   It was the way she pushed it aside got me.

DAISY  She'd had some port wine.

RAFE   I could see the rot setting in – because once she got away with it the others 'ud start, an' the next thing our mealtimes would be like feeding the monkeys at the zoo. I've seen homes like that. I know that in these days it's the fashion to give way to your children, but nobody's convinced me on that score yet.

DAISY  It must have seemed harsh to the poor girl.

RAFE   I agree – but I knew she'd her mother to fall back on and wouldn't go hungry. I may see her need, but I'd never see her bleed. I hope I'm not that heartless.

DAISY   Yes, but you know our Hilda's not one for giving way. She's as stubborn ...

RAFE   I know. She's as stubborn as her father.

RAFE *and* DAISY *clasp hands.*

They say the apple doesn't fall far from the tree, and I love her all the more for it, though I don't let her see it. But I had no choice over making a stand. If your children once beat you – you're licked for good. The young have no respect for weakness. And they're growing stronger as you're getting older. They soon take your measure. Why, even a six-months-old child knows when it's the boss.

FLORENCE *and* ARTHUR *are seen entering the front door.*

DAISY   It shouldn't be a battle, Dad – bringing up a family.

RAFE   I realize that now. Happen I started off on the wrong foot. 'Course when I look round at other families I begin to ask myself if there's a right foot. They seem no better than we are.

DAISY   Times have changed, Dad.

RAFE   Don't I know! When I was a lad the old and the young shared a world in common. But the young of today seem to think they have nothing at all in common with us. Well, I wonder.

FLORENCE *enters.* ARTHUR *follows, closing the door. They are both wearing suits.*

DAISY   (*rising*) Are you back, love? Hello Arthur.

FLORENCE   Hello, Mother. You beat us, Dad.

RAFE   Yes, Florence, I did.

DAISY   I'd better get the tea.

DAISY *goes to the kitchen.*

FLORENCE   (*taking off her jacket and putting it over a chair*) Had a good walk, Dad?

RAFE   I've done a few miles. I've been right across the moors and down by the Scotsman's Stump.

ARTHUR  It's lovely round there.

*HAROLD enters. He and* ARTHUR *nod to each other.*

RAFE  The air's like wine. What folk want to go abroad for I don't know. They seem to have no love or pride in their own countryside these days. Tramping those moors you get all sorts of ideas going through your head. (*Rising.*) That reminds me, I've had Handel's 'Largo' in my mind all afternoon.

*DAISY enters from the kitchen with a trolley.* HAROLD *goes to help her wheel it in.* RAFE *takes some music from the piano stool and sits at the piano.*

HAROLD  Hello, Arthur.

ARTHUR  Hello, Harold.

HAROLD  How's tricks?

ARTHUR  Very well, thank you.

HAROLD  Good, good. Here, left hand down a bit, Mother.

*HAROLD and* DAISY *lay out the salad plates on the table. Six plates have meat on them. The seventh,* HILDA'S, *is empty.* FLORENCE *switches on the centre and desk lights.* RAFE *plays the introduction, then stops.*

RAFE  Mother, it's been some time since we heard you sing.

DAISY  Ee, I'm rusty. I was just going to brew the tea.

RAFE  Tea can wait. Come on, Mother. (*He is quite infectious at these times.*) Let's have a bit of the old days ... (*He clears his throat.*)

*DAISY has no choice. She wipes her hands on her apron.* FLORENCE *is eager to join in and pulls* ARTHUR *in.* DAISY *beckons* HAROLD, *and he also joins in with a sigh. They all gather round the piano.* RAFE *has a good voice, and the singing is moving.*

ALL  (*singing*) Slumber, dear maid!

*During the song,* HILDA *enters from the kitchen, takes a paperback book from the desk, switches on the standard lamp and sits on the sofa, refusing to sing. A moment or two later* WILFRED *enters by the back door, then comes quietly in from the kitchen and sees the others gathered round the piano. He goes quietly to the fireplace, picks up the cat from the basket in which it has been sleeping unnoticed (or he brings the 'real' cat on with him), and creeps back to the kitchen. At the door, he turns to be sure that no one has seen him. A moment later he appears in the scullery carrying the cat and the herring. He puts them both outside the back door, hurries back to the living-room and joins loudly in the singing. He gets one or two glances from the others.*

Green boughs will cover thee,
Calm airs breathe over thee,
Where thou art laid.
Slumber, dear maid!
Green boughs will cover thee,
Calm airs breathe over thee,
Where thou art laid.
Slumber then peacefully,
O gentle maid!
Green boughs will cover thee,
Calm airs breathe over thee,
Where thou art laid.
Where thou art laid.

**WILFRED** Dad, you were in good voice.

HAROLD *moves to the table and continues laying.*

**RAFE** (*turning on the stool to face front and studying the music book*) Aye, you should always do a thing when the impulse is on you.

**WILFRED** That's what I always say, Dad.

**DAISY** I'll get the tea.

DAISY *goes to the kitchen.*

**WILFRED** I didn't know you could sing, Arthur.

**ARTHUR** Neither did I.

**RAFE** (*rising, singing*) King of Kings, hallelujah, bum, hallelujah, bum, bum, bum.

**ARTHUR** It's funny how you don't hear families singing these days.

**HAROLD** (*sitting in his place at the table*) Not unless they're drunk.

FLORENCE *gives the piano stool to* ARTHUR, *who places it at the table down stage left.*

**RAFE** It's like everything else – they want it done for 'em.

**FLORENCE**    Dad, remember they used to have lovely concerts at St Saviour's Hall?

**RAFE**    Aye, there was some good life in the town those days.

**HAROLD**    They've changed that into a bingo hall now. Chap that's taken it over has made a fortune.

    FLORENCE *goes to her place at the table.*

**RAFE**    Aye, the whole place is becoming a hive of bingo halls an' bettin' shops. Gambling will be the ruination of this country. It breaks my heart to see what moral decay a bit of prosperity brings with it.

**HAROLD**    I suppose it's every man to his taste...

**RAFE**    Don't talk daft. What sort of state do you think the world would be in if you left everybody to their taste? Just think of the things they'd get up to.

**WILFRED**    What things, Dad?

**RAFE**    You needn't ask. Haven't you read your *News of the World* today?

    WILFRED *moves away to the top of the table.*

    I know what I'd do in this country if I had my way.

**WILFRED**    (*affably*) What's that, Dad?

**RAFE**    I'd have every man, woman and child listen to the *Messiah* tonight. Just think of it – in every church and hall all over the country – listening to 'He Shall Feed His Flock'!

**ARTHUR**    Yes, but what good would that do?

**RAFE**    (*rising*) A great spiritual experience. People are starved in their souls. You'd waken up to a new civilization tomorrow.

    *He moves to his place above the table.*

**WILFRED**    'Course you would. Stands to reason.

**ARTHUR**    (*sitting on the piano stool*) What about them as didn't like it, Mr Crompton?

    DAISY *enters with the teapot and puts it on the table.* HILDA *rises and goes to her place. All except* RAFE *and* DAISY *sit.*

**RAFE**    It seems a hard thing to say, but you could dispense with 'em.

**DAISY**    Well, that seems to be everything.

RAFE    (*looking at* HILDA's *place*) Mother, I believe you've forgotten something.

DAISY    (*looking*) Oh, so I have! I'd forget my head if it was loose.

*DAISY goes to the kitchen.*

RAFE    A chap who remained unmoved after hearing 'I Know that My Redeemer Liveth' could hardly be moved if you gave him a whack with a fourteen-pound hammer.

WILFRED    (*laughing loudly*) You're a right comic, Dad.

*Everyone looks at WILFRED. RAFE sits above the table. DAISY enters with an empty plate, muttering.*

RAFE    Am I ...!

DAISY    (*to herself*) Ee, I don't know – that beats me! Where could it have got to? (*She gives* HAROLD *a look.*)

HAROLD    What're you staring at me for, Mum?

DAISY    I'm not staring at you.

HAROLD    Then I musta been staring at you.

RAFE    What's up, Mother?

DAISY    Our Hilda's herring ...

RAFE    Oh aye, what about it?

DAISY    I've just been for it and found it gone.

*There is a reaction at the table.*

RAFE    Gone? Gone where?

DAISY    Gone. It's disappeared. I think the cat must have got it.

RAFE    The cat! Got it off the shelf – how could it?

DAISY    Well, it's not on the plate. (*She has another look to make sure.*)

RAFE    Stop! (*Rising.*) Stop! I'm going to get to the bottom of this. Nobody start.

*RAFE goes to the kitchen, then enters the scullery.*

HAROLD    That cat better have nine lives.

*DAISY sits in her place at the table.*

ARTHUR    If I know anything it's going to lose one now.

WILFRED    He doesn't want to be too severe on it.

*Everyone looks at* WILFRED. RAFE *opens the back door,*

*goes outside, then returns holding the remains of the*
*herring. He takes it through into the living-room.*

**RAFE**    Anybody know anything about this?

**HAROLD**    Looks like the cat's been at it.

**WILFRED**    No doubt about it – I'd say.

**RAFE**    Aye, but who gave it to the cat? That's what I'm
going to find out.

**DAISY**    I don't suppose anybody gave it. It must have took
it.

**RAFE**    No cat of mine ever took things, unless they were
given 'em. They all knew better. (*He puts the bones
on the plate and replaces it in the kitchen.*)

**DAISY**    But it must have.

**FLORENCE**    It always has been a funny cat.

**RAFE**    Mother, when did you last see this herring?

**DAISY**    Do you mean before the cat took it?

**RAFE**    I mean before it disappeared.

**DAISY**    I saw it just before I made the salad. I left the
herring in the kitchen because I thought it wouldn't
look so nice on the table. When I was going back in
the kitchen you asked me to join in the singing, and
I did. That's when it must have grabbed it.

**RAFE**    We'll come to when it grabbed it later. (*He turns to*
FLORENCE *and* ARTHUR.) Now then, you two were
singing?

**FLORENCE**    But of course, Dad.

**ARTHUR**    I was doing my best.

**RAFE**    (*to* HAROLD) How about you?

**HAROLD**    I was yodelling away.

**RAFE**    (*to* HILDA) How about you? You were sat across
there. (*He wipes his hands on his napkin.*)

**DAISY**    (*interposing*) It couldn't have been our Hilda.

**RAFE**    Why not?

**DAISY**    Because she said something to me before tea which
meant she would never do that.

**RAFE**    I see. (*To* WILFRED.) Now, that just leaves you, then.

**HAROLD**    I don't think it was our Wilf.

| | |
|---|---|
| **RAFE** | How do you know? |
| **HAROLD** | Well, because ... |
| **WILFRED** | Thanks, Harold. I was singing, Dad. You must have heard me. You all heard me singing, didn't you? |
| **ARTHUR** | Yes – I did, Wilf. |
| **WILFRED** | Thanks, Arthur. |
| **HAROLD** | So did I ... |
| **RAFE** | Didn't I see you go into the kitchen? |
| **WILFRED** | (*rising*) No, you didn't, I – oh, I'm sorry, I'm telling a lie. I did. Sorry, Dad. I went into the kitchen to get a drink of water – that was it. I remember now. (*He sits again.*) |
| **RAFE** | You went to get a drink of water just before your tea? |
| **WILFRED** | I always have a drink of water just before my tea, don't I, Mum? It gives me an appetite. You've seen me, haven't you, Harold? |
| **HAROLD** | Many a time. Come on, Mum, start pouring out the tea. We don't want an inquest on the herring. |
| **RAFE** | (*to* HAROLD) It's an inquest on the truth. And don't you try to override me. (*To* WILFRED.) Then you were the last in the kitchen? |
| **WILFRED** | I don't think so. 'Course, I might have been. Was I, Mum? |
| **DAISY** | No, love, I think it was me. |
| **WILFRED** | There you are, Dad. I mean Mum wouldn't give the herring to the cat, and neither would I. |
| **HILDA** | I was last in the kitchen. |
| **RAFE** | You be quiet, please. |
| **WILFRED** | (*rising*) I know that cat, Dad, it's a right thief. 'Course you can't blame 'em – it's their nature. And they've got to follow their own natures. |
| **RAFE** | (*moving down stage; to* WILFRED) Come here! |

WILFRED *rises and moves down.* DAISY *touches his hand as he passes.*

I'm going to ask you a question. All I want to know

is the truth, so be careful how you answer. Did you give that herring to the cat?

**WILFRED** Me? Why should I? I didn't have to eat it, did I? Anyway, I like herrings. Don't I, Mum?

**DAISY** 'Course you do, love.

**RAFE** Answer me, did you give that herring to the cat?

**WILFRED** I wouldn't do a thing like that, Dad. Would I, Mum? Knowing what store Dad had set on it.

ARTHUR, *upset, is about to interfere, but* FLORENCE *detains him.* HILDA *tries to persuade him with a look.*

**DAISY** Of course you wouldn't, love.

**RAFE** Just hold your hands out, will you?

**WILFRED** What – what for?

**RAFE** Just put them out, please.

*Only with great difficulty can* WILFRED *get himself to hold out his hands.* RAFE *bends and sniffs at* WILFRED'S *fingers.* WILFRED *looks very nervous.* RAFE *knows something, but keeps it to himself.*

Now, for the last time, answer me – did you give that herring to the cat?

**WILFRED** Me? Certainly not! Positively not, as they say. I could swear to it – I could, honest ...

**RAFE** Oh – you could swear to it, could you? I see ... (*He moves to the piano and picks up the Bible.*)

*Everyone watches* RAFE *with stunned amazement.*

**DAISY** No – no – Dad – not the Bible – you can't make him ...

RAFE *waves* DAISY *and the others to silence.* ARTHUR *looks as though he might protest.*

**HAROLD** This is not right, Mum.

**RAFE** I'm going to get to the bottom of this. (*To* WILFRED.) Take this holy book in your hand.

**WILFRED** (*aghast at the idea*) No, no, Dad. I couldn't. Don't ask me ...

**HAROLD** I think we've gone far enough.

**RAFE** Take it when I tell you. Take it...

**WILFRED** No – no, Dad ...

RAFE    Take it! I never turn back once I start something.
        (*He thrusts the Bible on* WILFRED.) Hold it up – up!
        WILFRED *looks to his mother.*

WILFRED Mum – don't let him make me ...

FLORENCE (*appealing*) Dad – you know you'll be sorry if you
        go too far.

RAFE    You can't go too far in finding the truth. (*Raising a
        hand for* DAISY *to be silent.*) Now swear solemnly ...

WILFRED No! I can't.

ARTHUR  Don't press the lad any more, Mr Crompton.
        HILDA *watches* RAFE *with hatred.* RAFE *gives* ARTHUR *a
        look.*

RAFE    Be quiet, please.

FLORENCE Wilf, love – say if you have ...

RAFE    Now hold that book up – high – higher!

WILFRED It would be wrong – swearing on God's Bible about
        a thing like that. Wouldn't it, Mum? Eh, Florence?

DAISY   Dad, don't force that good book on him. Let the lad
        tell you in his own way.

RAFE    He's told me in his own way. I will not harbour a
        liar under my roof. (*Obsessively.*) I must have the
        truth! It's the only way to live – by the truth.

DAISY   Don't press him too far, Dad – you know ...

RAFE    I only want the truth. I'll not give way on that.

HILDA   Stop him, Mum – It's not right...

RAFE    Lift it up – up – higher. I'm determined to get the
        truth ...
        WILFRED *holds the Bible up in trembling hands.*
        Now say, I swear by Almighty God ...

WILFRED No! No! No, Dad ..

HAROLD  You can't have a bloody inquisition over a herring.

RAFE    It's over nothing but the truth.

HAROLD  Then if you want to know the truth I'll tell you – I
        gave that herring to the cat.

WILFRED (*with a cry*) No! No, no, I must tell you – it were ...
        *He swoons.*
        *Everyone rises.*

**HILDA**    (*with a scream*) Wilf! Mum, he's having one of his turns ...
*RAFE quickly catches* WILFRED *as he falls.*

**DAISY**    Don't let him fall ...

**RAFE**    I've got him, Mother – now don't get excited. (*He slowly lets* WILFRED *down.*) Open the window, somebody. Bring some cold water.
ARTHUR *crosses and opens the window.* HAROLD *goes to the kitchen for water.*

**DAISY**    (*moving to* WILFRED) My little boy – he's all of a sweat. (*She kneels beside* WILFRED. *To* RAFE.) You pressed him too far.

**HILDA**    (*moving to above* WILFRED) Wilf, love – are you...

**RAFE**    He'll be all right – the water. (*He rises left of* WILFRED.)

**DAISY**    I'll unfasten his collar.

**HILDA**    (*to* RAFE) Oh, you – you – look what you've done to him – (*picking up the Bible*) – you and your truth. I hate you – I could ... (*She raises the Bible to strike* RAFE.)
FLORENCE *takes the Bible from* HILDA *and replaces it on the piano.* HAROLD *enters with a glass of water.*
Oh, you brute – I'll not stay another minute under your roof. I'm going, Mum. Take care of our Wilf. (*She kisses* DAISY.) I'll never come back to this rotten prison.
HILDA *goes out slamming the door.*

**DAISY**    Hilda!

**HAROLD**    (*handing* DAISY *the water*) Here y'are, Mum.

**DAISY**    He's coming round. Here, take this water, love.
RAFE *comes back to himself after his shock.*

**RAFE**    Mind yourself, Mother – let me do it. You're spilling it.
*He tends* WILFRED, *then hands the water to* HAROLD.
HAROLD *goes to the kitchen with the water.*

**RAFE**    How do you feel, son?

**WILFRED**    Did I have one of my ...?

**DAISY**    Just a little one, love.

**WILFRED**    Let me get up. (*He rises.*)

**RAFE**    Easy does it. Bide you there, where there's some air.

DAISY *takes him to the sofa.* RAFE *moves the chairs in
to make room.*

WILFRED    I thought I heard our Hilda shouting.

RAFE    Rest yourself, lad. Mother, shall we all get back to
tea?

DAISY    (*to* WILFRED) Will you be all right, love?

HAROLD *enters from the kitchen.*

WILFRED    'Course I will, Mum. It's been a long time since I
had one of them. Carry on, everybody. Sorry about
that herring, Dad. It was me. I felt I couldn't bear to
see it put in front of our Hilda again.

*All except* ARTHUR *return to their places round the
table.*

RAFE    It's all right – now you've told me. We'll not
mention it any more.

DAISY *pours tea.*

HAROLD    Come on, Arthur, don't hang fire.

ARTHUR    Mother, don't pour any for me, please.

DAISY    Why not, love?

RAFE    Sit down, Arthur – and have your tea.

ARTHUR    No thank you, Mr Crompton.

HAROLD    He'll have a cup of tea, Mum.

ARTHUR    No, I won't ..

FLORENCE    Why – what's up, Arthur?

RAFE    I think he's got something on his mind.

ARTHUR    Yes, I have. What your Wilfred did – and your Hilda
– they did out of love – love for one another – and
they showed some spirit ...

FLORENCE    Arthur!

ARTHUR    But you want to crush the spirit out of everybody
who doesn't agree with you. You know what you
are, Mr Crompton?

FLORENCE    Be quiet, Arthur.

ARTHUR    You're a bully ...

RAFE    Oh ...!

ARTHUR    Only a bully could have done what you've just
done. (*To* DAISY.) I'm sorry, Mother – I had to come
out with it.

DAISY    All right, Arthur.

**FLORENCE**  I think you've said enough.

**RAFE**  Nay, don't stop him – I'm learning.

**ARTHUR**  You'll never learn – not so long as you ram your own way down everybody's throat. You make out you help 'em – but you only belittle 'em.

**RAFE**  Have you done?

**ARTHUR**  No. You used that Holy Bible for your own ends.

**RAFE**  I used it to find out the truth.

**ARTHUR**  The truth was staring you in the face – but you couldn't see it. You used it to satisfy your suspicious mind! My folk are nothing, but they would never even dare to do a thing like that. Yet you set yourself up as God-fearing! I used to respect you, but now I see you're nothing but a tyrant!

**FLORENCE**  Arthur!

**ARTHUR**  And another thing – you'd no right to let that little girl go off like that.

**RAFE**  Oh – why not?

**ARTHUR**  You wouldn't understand if I told you. (*To* DAISY.) I'm right sorry, Mother. Goodbye, everybody. Florence, are you ready?

**FLORENCE**  Ready? What for?

**ARTHUR**  What do you think? To come with me.

**FLORENCE**  But I ...

**ARTHUR**  (*gently*) Now I'm afraid you'll have to make your mind up one way or the other. It's come to that.
FLORENCE *looks at* RAFE.

**RAFE**  Aye, Florence, but you know what it'll mean if you go ...
FLORENCE *looks at* RAFE, *then at* ARTHUR. *She hesitates, then swiftly rises and picks up her jacket. She kisses* DAISY *and* WILFRED, *and puts her hand on* HAROLD'S *shoulder.*

**HAROLD**  God bless, love.
FLORENCE *lets out an unexpected stifled sob and moves towards the door.* ARTHUR *takes her and goes out with her.*

*The* CURTAIN *falls*

SCENE TWO

*The same. Monday morning.*

*When the curtain rises, the stage is empty. The radio is playing the final tune of 'Housewives' Choice'. The front door is slightly ajar.* BETSY JANE *is seen approaching it. She enters and calls.*

BETSY JANE  (*off*) Daisy! Daisy! (*She appears in the doorway, calling upstairs.*) Daisy, are you there? (*She comes into the living-room.*)
DAISY *enters through the back door with her basket of washing and dumps it on the washing-machine. 'Housewives' Choice' finishes on the radio. Sombre music is followed by a voice announcing, 'It's five to ten.'* BETSY JANE *hurriedly switches it off.* DAISY *enters the living-room from the kitchen.*

DAISY  Don't mind me. You're an early caller.
BETSY JANE  You left your front door open. Did you know?
DAISY  Yes, I'd a very special reason. Well, have you got my five pounds?
BETSY JANE  You're not skint, are you?
DAISY  Yes, I am.
BETSY JANE  Well, it's like this – Connie Clarke's mail order firm have let me down. I'd ordered a seven-day striking clock with Westminster chimes from them, which should have arrived this morning.
DAISY  What's that got to do with my money?
BETSY JANE  I'd arranged to flog it to Mrs Clegg for five pounds cash. It'll cost me seven pound ten, in instalments, of course, so it's a bargain all round. But the damn thing hasn't arrived yet. It might come by the afternoon post, and I swear on my dying ...

DAISY    Don't swear! Just you bring it. I can't tell you the worry it's caused me.

BETSY JANE    Leave it to me, Daisy; I'll not let you down. You look tired.

DAISY    I didn't sleep all that well last night.

BETSY JANE    You're a clannish lot, you Cromptons!

DAISY    In what way?

BETSY JANE    You might have your troubles amongst yourselves, but you don't like it to go outside your four walls. You stick together as a family – I will say that for you.

DAISY    What are you getting at?

BETSY JANE    Your Hilda is just the same. She didn't want to say a word.

DAISY    (*rising*) Is she all right? Have you seen her?

BETSY JANE    She's all right. Yon chap found her wandering about along the canal path. He brought her back and she spent the night with us. I got it out of her, though. Open confession is good for the soul. How you've been able to put up with that flaming husband of yours these past thirty years, I do not know! Mine's bad enough – but at least he's got the virtue of being stupid. I'll fetch her in. (*She moves to the front door and gives a whistling call off.*) Come on, love, the coast is clear! (*She pokes her head into the room.*) I'll leave you with her.

    BETSY JANE *goes out through the front door.* DAISY *smooths her face and hair to recover her motherly look.* HILDA *enters hesitantly, looks at* DAISY, *then runs into her arms, sobbing.*

DAISY    (*hugging her*) There, there, there, are you all right, love? Ee, I'm right glad to see you.

    HILDA *breaks free and wipes her eyes.*

HILDA    I'm sorry, Mum, I am a softie.

DAISY    It'll do you good, love, a cry. Hold on a tick. Kettle's boiling.

    (DAISY *goes to the kitchen.* HILDA *moves up to the door.*) (*From the kitchen.*) So you didn't go to work today, love?

HILDA      No. Betsy Jane didn't wake me. I don't think I could
           have faced my mates at work if she had. I feel I can
           never face them again. You know, I used always be
           boasting about my dad.
           DAISY *enters with a small tray on which are two cups
           and a jar of instant coffee. She gives the tray to* HILDA.
DAISY      You'll get over it, love. How was it at Betsy Jane's?
           DAISY *goes back into the kitchen.*
HILDA      They're a mucky lot, Mum. Good-hearted – ee, but I
           couldn't live there. She's got that enamel teapot on
           the hob beside the fire all the time. You can hear
           the tea sizzling and stewing inside. It would make
           you sick.
           DAISY *enters with a kettle of boiling water and a jug
           of milk.*
DAISY      Well, you get used to your own home. It's in the
           nature of things. (*She sits in* RAFE'S *armchair.*)
HILDA      In fact, I felt sick this morning before I even tasted it.
DAISY      (*reacts*) Did you now!
HILDA      I hope my dad doesn't take that herring out on our
           Wilf.
DAISY      (*making coffee*) You know your father never bears
           grudges – once he's rooted out things – except
           against himself. Our Florence went off with Arthur. I
           wish you'd seen that! It quite touched me, the
           courage he showed in standing up to your dad. I
           sometimes wish I'd shown a bit more. (*She holds
           out the kettle.*)
HILDA      (*placing the kettle in the fireplace and then sitting*) I
           don't know how you put up with him, Mum.
DAISY      (*handing* HILDA *her cup*) You can always put up
           with somebody – so long as you know they're
           genuine.
HILDA      But look how he domineers you.
DAISY      Well, if he weren't doing that he'd be doing
           something else.
HILDA      And yet he used to be so understanding. I wonder
           what's made him change?
DAISY      Are you sure it's him that's changed, love?

BETSY JANE *enters.*

**BETSY JANE** It's only me. Oh, you've got the coffee on the go. (*She sniffs.*) Doesn't it smell nice!
(DAISY *gives her a look, then rises and goes to the kitchen.*)
(*Moving to* HILDA.) Was she very upset?

**HILDA** I haven't been able to tell her yet.

**BETSY JANE** It'll give her a shock.

DAISY *enters with a cup.*

**DAISY** What's that?

**BETSY JANE** Your Hilda has some news for you.

**DAISY** (*putting the cup on the tray and picking up the kettle*) Not bad, I hope? (*To* HILDA.) What is it, love? (*She moves towards* HILDA.)

**HILDA** (*rising and moving away*) I'm getting out of it, Mum – I'm going away.

**DAISY** Ee, for the moment I thought it was something worse.

**HILDA** Worse? What?

**DAISY** Nothing, love. Away? Where to?

**BETSY JANE** She's going up the smoke – to London. (*She takes the kettle, fills her cup, and replaces the kettle.*)

**DAISY** Ee, you aren't, are you, love – going so far away?

**HILDA** Yes, Mum, I'm going tonight.

**BETSY JANE** Women bus conductors can earn fourteen pound a week.

**DAISY** You don't want to go, do you, love, to London – a big strange city like that?

**HILDA** I want to get away, Mum. I don't feel I can face folk here any more. I used to feel so proud of our home – but now ...

**BETSY JANE** (*spooning coffee in her cup*) I've been telling her – she can't go to London without money in her pocket. (*She notices the sugar is absent and fetches it from the kitchen.*)

**HILDA** Can you lend me some, Mum?

**DAISY** Lend you – well, I'll have to scratch around a bit.

**HILDA** (*putting her cup on the table*) Don't worry, Mum, if you can't, I'll manage somehow. I've got my factory savings, but it takes a fortnight to get the money through. I'll go to Vy Hopkins – you know – who worked at our place. I can see you're worrying – now I'll manage one way or another. (*She takes two records from the rack.*)

DAISY  Ee, love, I don't like the thought of it.

HILDA  I hate the idea – but I feel I must do it. Now I'll just go upstairs and collect a few bits of things.

DAISY  Aye, but leave some behind...

BETSY JANE  Just in case you change your mind.

HILDA  I'm not likely to do that.

DAISY  I shan't feel you're gone the same – if I see your things around.

HILDA  Don't worry about the money, Mum, if it's an awkward time.

HILDA *goes out.*

DAISY  Her father's favourite – and look what he's driven her to! (*Going to her handbag on the sideboard.*) She can't go to London broke. She must have something.

BETSY JANE  (*putting her cup on the tray*) Aye, she'd be easy prey for all them pimps they've got down there – they're on the lookout for her sort.

DAISY  Do you think for certain you'll have that money for me today?

BETSY JANE  I hope so – but I couldn't say for certain. You know what the post is getting like these days.

DAISY  I've got to lay my hands on something for her. (*She moves to the desk and tries in vain to open it.*)

BETSY JANE  Is there some money in there?

DAISY  Yes, quite a lot.

BETSY JANE  And you can't get at it? He's got the key, eh? (*She joins* DAISY *at the desk and tries to open it.*) So near and yet so far.

DAISY  The girl's got to have some money. Do you know where I can borrow some?

BETSY JANE  Yes, but not without your husband's signature. They've got you every road. It's a man's world all right. (*Inspecting the lock.*) Have you got a bit of

|  | wire? I might be able to pick this lock for you. |
| ---: | :--- |
| DAISY | What kind of wire? |
| BETSY JANE | Forget it – this hairpin will do. (*She begins to pick the lock.*) I used to be quite good at it. My mother showed me how to do it. She used to say to carry out a wife's job you can't know too much. |
| DAISY | Is there anything I could pawn? |
| BETSY JANE | Would he miss the piano? (*She continues picking.*) |
| DAISY | Here – what are you up to? |
| BETSY JANE | You're behind the times. There used to be fifty pawnbrokers in town, and now there's only two. They say there's more money about these days but it never comes my way. It's nothing when you have it, and all the world when you haven't. |
| DAISY | Here, be careful. Mind you don't scratch it. |
| BETSY JANE | I'd scratch him if I got half a chance. There is one pawnbroker I know – in fact I've my ring in hock there at present. I keep telling yon chap I've mislaid it. (*She chuckles.*) Damn fools, men. You can tell 'em anything. I always feel it's a pity to tell 'em the truth. They don't believe you in any case. |
| DAISY | Leave it alone, please. I don't want you to tinker with it. Besides, you'll never open it. |

BETSY JANE *fiddles and tugs, and suddenly the lid springs open.*

|  |  |
| ---: | :--- |
| BETSY JANE | You're too late! I bloody have. Practice makes perfect. |
| DAISY | Oh, my God! |
| BETSY JANE | All done by kindness, here's the lolly. (*She grabs the box, then picks it up with her apron.*) Mustn't leave fingerprints. |
| DAISY | Put it back! |
| BETSY JANE | (*crossing* DAISY *to the table*) Put it back! – are you mad? What about your Hilda? Besides, once I get my fingers on it I'll be able to pay you back the five quid I owe you. Now, where's the key for it? |

| | |
|---|---|
| **DAISY** | (*searching the desk*) The key! I forgot, he must have it with him. |
| **BETSY JANE** | Can you beat it! After all my trouble. It'll take two pounds of gelignite to burst this flamin' thing open. |
| **DAISY** | (*turning with a paper-knife in her hand*) Can't you open it with a hairpin? |
| **BETSY JANE** | Hairpin? Who the hell do you think I am – Houdini? Give me that thing – it's got a sharp point. |
| **DAISY** | (*giving* BETSY JANE *the paper-knife*) Go careful now. |
| **BETSY JANE** | What are you worried about – me or the bloody paper-knife? |
| **DAISY** | Don't ruin it. |
| **BETSY JANE** | If I had him here, I'd ruin him! (*She tries with the knife.*) Dammit, it won't go in. (*She puts the knife down and raises the box above her head.*) Stand back – I'll burst it open! |
| **DAISY** | No, no! |
| **BETSY JANE** | Don't get excited – I'm only coddin'. |
| **DAISY** | Quick, put it back, put it back! |
| **BETSY JANE** | What's up? What are you getting so nervous about? Anybody would think it was the holy of holies. |
| | DAISY *has a sudden realization of what she is doing, grabs the box and knife from* BETSY JANE, *puts them back in the desk and shuts the lid.* |
| **DAISY** | No! I can't bear the thought of what I'm up to. |
| **BETSY JANE** | It's what he's driven you to. |
| **DAISY** | Quick, lock it. He'd never forgive me. |
| **BETSY JANE** | (*crossing to the desk*) Lock it? How can I? I've got no key. |
| **DAISY** | You opened it. |
| **BETSY JANE** | You can't lock 'em as easy. Now what are you going to do about your Hilda? |
| **DAISY** | There must be something I could give you to pawn as wouldn't be missed for a day or two – I could get round it somehow. |

**BETSY JANE**    Well, it'll have to be summat special. Pawnbrokers are very choosy these days.

**DAISY**    Hold on a tick – I think I've got the very thing. Here, wait out the back for me – I don't want our Hilda to see.

DAISY *goes out.*

**BETSY JANE**    I wish I lived here. I'd have that box open if it were the last thing I did.

BETSY JANE *goes to the kitchen, then enters the scullery and stands near the back door.* DAISY *hurries in carrying something on a coat-hanger which is covered with a white dust sheet.* BETSY JANE *waits near the back door as* DAISY *goes through the kitchen and into the scullery.*

Now what have you got there?

DAISY *removes the dust sheet and hold up* RAFE'S *new overcoat.*

Ee, that's a grand coat.

**DAISY**    How much do you think you could get me on it?

**BETSY JANE**    Whose is it?

**DAISY**    It's Rafe's. Never been worn. Only got it last Friday. Cost thirty-two guineas.

**BETSY JANE**    You're never going to pop it?

**DAISY**    Can you get me ten pounds on it?

**BETSY JANE**    (*taking the coat*) Ee, it feels like velvet. He knows what's good – I'll say that for him.

**DAISY**    I durst not think of the shock he'd get if he knew I'd do a thing like this behind his back.

**BETSY JANE**    (*rolling the coat up*) It might do him all the good in the world. It would let him see what scheming his wife has to do to get ten rotten quid for his daughter, and him having all that money locked away there under his nose. It's bloody men all over.

DAISY *pushes* BETSY JANE *out with the coat, as —*

*The* CURTAIN *falls*

*The same. Monday evening.*

*When the curtain rises,* WILFRED *is seated at the piano playing a Chopin Nocturne.* HAROLD *is at the table, very much aware of himself, brushing crumbs off the tablecloth into a crumb tray. There is a knock at the front door.*

HAROLD    Somebody at the door, Wilf.

WILFRED    Then, why don't you go and answer it?

HAROLD    Me? I can't do two jobs at once. Besides, it might be our Hilda.
    WILFRED *stops playing and quickly goes to open the front door.* HAROLD *looks for somewhere to throw the crumbs, aims under the armchair, then throws the tray in the sideboard drawer, folds the tablecloth carefully, concertinas it, and shoves it in the drawer.* BETSY JANE *enters, carrying a purse.* WILFRED *follows her.*

BETSY JANE    Is your mother in?
    HAROLD *places the runner and bowl of hyacinths on the table.*

WILFRED    (*closing the door*) She's washing up the tea things. Don't say you've brought that five quid back at last!

BETSY JANE    That's all been arranged between your mother and me.

WILFRED    Glad to hear it. I'll go and tell her you're here.
    WILFRED *goes to the kitchen.*

BETSY JANE    (*sniffing*) There's a funny atmosphere in here.

HAROLD    Well, it was all right. (*He sits and picks up the evening paper.*)

BETSY JANE    It feels like a morgue.

HAROLD    I wouldn't know. I've never been in one.

| | |
|---|---|
| **BETSY JANE** | Don't give up hope. (*She sits by the table and looks round.*) Where is he? |
| **HAROLD** | The old chap? He's upstairs. He's wandering about like a man lost. |
| **BETSY JANE** | That'll be a change. |
| | WILFRED *enters from the kitchen.* |
| **WILFRED** | She says you'd better go in to her. |
| **BETSY JANE** | (*rising*) Right. |
| | BETSY JANE *goes to the kitchen.* |
| **HAROLD** | We could do with getting the old chap out of the way. |
| **WILFRED** | Aye, the girls'll be coming around. Can't you come up with something to get him out? |
| **HAROLD** | I'll try. You never think you'd miss 'em that much. |
| **WILFRED** | Aye, even our Florence! If it's only for her bossing. |
| **HAROLD** | Know what – I feel the time's getting ripe for us to move off with 'em – what do you say? |
| **WILFRED** | I'd say you were a bit too fond of Mum's cooking. |
| **HAROLD** | If I once set my mind on leaving, nothing will hold me. And it won't take much. |
| | WILFRED *sits at the piano and plays quietly.* HAROLD *goes back to his paper.* DAISY *enters the scullery with* BETSY JANE, *and they go to the back door.* DAISY *switches on the scullery light.* |
| **BETSY JANE** | I knew you'd be worrying. |
| **DAISY** | I'm glad you got the ten pounds for it. |
| **BETSY JANE** | Yes – but I only got nine pounds fourteen in cash. Know what they charge for a pawn-ticket on that amount? Five bob! Used to be tuppence. |
| **DAISY** | Thanks, Betsy Jane. |
| **BETSY JANE** | An' yon pawnbroker charges a shilling extra for putting the coat on a hanger – keeps the creases out, see. I thought he rated that. Count it to make sure it's right. |
| | RAFE *enters, wearing slippers and a cardigan. He sees* BETSY JANE *in the scullery, and sits in his armchair.* |
| **DAISY** | I trust you. |

| | |
|---|---|
| **BETSY JANE** | Thank you. Well, same as I say about the other, as soon as that Westminster chiming clock arrives I'll ... |
| **DAISY** | Yes, I'd be very glad if you would. |
| **BETSY JANE** | Ee, Daisy, you look years older than when I came in last Friday tea-time. |
| **DAISY** | Yes – and I feel it. |
| **BETSY JANE** | Well, try not to worry. It'll not always be dark at seven. Has he tried his bureau yet? |
| **DAISY** | Don't remind me of it, I've enough on my mind. |
| **BETSY JANE** | Yon chap of mine isn't home from work yet. What pests men are! They're either missing from home or for ever under your feet! |

BETSY JANE *goes out through the back door.* HAROLD *points to the paper.* WILFRED *turns his head and sees him.*

| | |
|---|---|
| **HAROLD** | (*reading the paper excitedly*) Hy, Dad, you've missed something good tonight. |

DAISY *switches off the scullery light and goes into the kitchen.* WILFRED *stops playing and rises.*

| | |
|---|---|
| **RAFE** | Have I now! What's that? |
| **HAROLD** | The *Messiah* – at Manchester. Handel's *Messiah*. |
| **RAFE** | Nay, that's not tonight – that's Easter Monday. |
| **HAROLD** | Oh, no, Dad, it's tonight at seven-thirty – Huddersfield Choral Society. Look, there! What can't speak, can't lie! (*He takes the paper to* RAFE *and points.*) |
| **WILFRED** | (*moving down to* HAROLD) By gum, you're right, Harold! Fancy that! |

DAISY *enters from the kitchen, switching off the light. She looks at the desk, then crosses to the sideboard to put the money from* BETSY JANE *into her handbag.*

| | |
|---|---|
| **RAFE** | I wish you'd told me earlier. |

WILFRED *moves up from the piano.*

| | |
|---|---|
| **HAROLD** | You could still make it. |
| **DAISY** | You what? |
| **WILFRED** | The *Messiah* – at Manchester. |

DAISY *looks puzzled.*

| | |
|---|---|
| **RAFE** | (*rising*) I thought it were next week, Mother. I don't know what's come over me lately. (*He hands the paper back to* HAROLD.) |
| | HAROLD *sits.* |
| | I've got our suitcase down from the top of the wardrobe. When they come to collect their things you'll let me know, will you? I'd rather not be around. |
| **DAISY** | All right, Dad. |
| | RAFE *takes his bunch of keys from his pocket.* DAISY *watches apprehensively.* |
| **RAFE** | I expect you'll be needing some extra money now – with all this coming and going. |
| **DAISY** | (*barring* RAFE'S *way to the desk*) No, no, Dad – it's all right. |
| **RAFE** | Are you sure? |
| **DAISY** | Positive. I'll manage. |
| **WILFRED** | You could still get to Manchester in time, Dad. |
| **HAROLD** | Aye, Dad – there's a marvellous bus service. Better still, you could even catch a train ... |
| **RAFE** | (*moving to the fireplace*) I don't think I'll bother now. |
| **WILFRED** | You could be door to door in what – forty minutes. |
| **HAROLD** | Thirty-five with a bit of luck. |
| **RAFE** | You two seem to want to get me out of the way. |
| **HAROLD** | No, no. It's just that we know how you enjoy it. |
| **WILFRED** | It would take you out of yourself, Dad. |
| **RAFE** | What time did you say it starts? |
| **HAROLD** | (*looking in the paper*) Seven-thirty.'Course, they're always a bit late striking up. |
| **RAFE** | I think I will go after all. What d'you say, Mother? I'd like to get out. |
| **DAISY** | What's that, Dad? |
| **RAFE** } (*together*) | The *Messiah.* |
| **HAROLD** | The *Messiah* – at Manchester. |
| **DAISY** | Oh, I see. It might do you good, the change, Dad – but will you have time? |
| **WILFRED** | (*cutting in*) 'Course he'll have time. |
| **HAROLD** | Sure he'll have time. |

DAISY   Can I help you? You'll have to hurry.

RAFE    I'll just get the jacket to these trousers – and my black shoes.

WILFRED I'll get your jacket, Dad.

WILFRED *goes out.*

HAROLD  Let me get your shoes, Dad.

HAROLD *goes to the kitchen.*

DAISY   Is there anything you'd like me to say to them, Dad? When they call round? I mean – the girls.

RAFE    Aye, there's a lot, Mother – but I'm afraid nothing as would be of any use. Two good daughters – it takes you half a lifetime to bring 'em up – and you lose them in a couple of minutes. (*He goes quiet as the kitchen door opens.*)

HAROLD *enters with* RAFE'S *shoes* .

HAROLD  It's better than seeing it on the telly, eh, Dad? (*He pulls* RAFE'S *cardigan off and puts it on a chair.*)

RAFE    (*sitting on his chair to change his slippers*) Eh? Seeing it? Seeing's nothing – hearing's nothing. It's the participation. You've got to enter into the *Messiah.*

WILFRED *enters with* RAFE'S *jacket and puts it on the chair arm.* RAFE *puts his slippers down.* DAISY *moves to the desk.*

HAROLD  Oh, I see what you mean, Dad.

RAFE    I don't think you do, lad. It's a going out of yourself and entering into a new world. I don't think you've tried it yet. (*He rises, puts on his jacket and looks in the mirror.*)

DAISY   I'll get your coat, Dad.

DAISY *goes out.*

HAROLD  (*looking out of the window*) Aye, it'll be cold coming home.

WILFRED Hy, Dad! A good idea – how about your new coat?

HAROLD  Good old Wilf! It'd be favourite tonight!

DAISY *enters with* RAFE'S *old coat, scarf and cap.*
What do you say, Mum?

DAISY   What's that?

WILFRED   My dad's new overcoat. Don't you think he should
          wear it tonight?

RAFE      Stop fussing. I'll be all right as I am.

DAISY     Let your dad please himself.

WILFRED   I thought it'd be a good christening for it, Dad – the
          *Messiah*.

HAROLD    Aye, a good idea, Wilf. I'll go and get it, eh, Dad?
          (*He opens the door wide.*)

RAFE      (*moving back to the fireplace*) Your mother's got me
          this one now. So shut up about the new overcoat.

HAROLD    (*moving down stage*) Please yourself, Dad.
          DAISY *helps* RAFE *to put on his coat.*

RAFE      (*adjusting the coat*) There's nowt wrong with this.

DAISY     P'raps you'll feel more at home in it. (*Moving up
          stage.*) Now don't get yourself late.

WILFRED   (*pointing*) Hy, Dad – you've got a button missing!

RAFE      Never! Where?

WILFRED   In the middle – look, right in the front.

RAFE      Bless my soul, so I have.

HAROLD    It's a sign, Dad. You should have put your new one
          on.

RAFE      Mother, what have you been up to?

DAISY     (*moving down stage*) What? What do you mean?

RAFE      A button missing off my coat – that's not like you.

WILFRED   I'll run and fetch your new one, Dad.

RAFE      I'll be all right in this.

WILFRED   It'll not take me a tick, Dad.

RAFE      I tell you I'll be all right in this. Nobody's going to
          notice a button.

WILFRED   Sorry, Dad.

RAFE      You meant well, son. I'm sorry to bite your head off.
          Go on, off with you upstairs and fetch it.

WILFRED   Right, Dad ...

DAISY     (*shouting*) No, no – don't go. It's no use.
          *They all go silent and look at her.*

HAROLD    What's no use?

RAFE    (*taking off his coat*) What's up, Mother?

DAISY   (*recovering*) It's no use him going – I'll go – I know where it is.

HAROLD  Let me go, Mum. Save yourself. (*He starts to move.*)

DAISY   No! I tell you, no – why do you keep interfering? *They all go silent* .

RAFE    To save any bother, I'll go and get it myself. (*He gives his coat to* DAISY, *then turns.*) Mother, you're not yourself this evening. Keep calm – have faith. (*He gives her arm a comforting squeeze.*)

        RAFE *goes out to the stairs.* DAISY *watches after him.* WILFRED *and* HAROLD *look at her and then at each other.*

WILFRED Mum, suppose I nip into Betsy Jane's and bring our Hilda back – as soon as he goes?

        DAISY *does not appear to hear him.*

HAROLD  Aye, you do that, Wilf.

WILFRED And you go down to Arthur's an' collect him an' Florence. I'll get your jacket. (*He goes through to the scullery, collects his and* HAROLD'S *jackets from the back door, and returns to the living-room.*)

HAROLD  All right. (*He puts his arms around* DAISY.) We'll go and see what's happening. We won't be long, Mum. I don't like to see you worried.

WILFRED We'll nip back in the minute we see him go up the street.

RAFE    (*off*) Where've you put it, Mother?

HAROLD  Now don't let yourself get upset, Mum.

WILFRED It'll be all right.

RAFE    (*off*) I can't see it.

DAISY   You go off now.

WILFRED Not be long. God bless.

        WILFRED *and* HAROLD *put their jackets on, exchanging glances of concern.*

HAROLD  See you soon. It'll all come right.

        HAROLD *and* WILFRED *go out and through the front door.*

RAFE (*off*) Mother! Mother! Where have you put my new
overcoat? It's not in the wardrobe. Can you come
and help me find it, love, or I'll be late.

DAISY *moves about in desperation. She throws* RAFE'S
*clothes on the hallstand, grabs her handbag, throws
it on the table, then crosses to the desk, flings the lid
down, and covers her face.*

DAISY I knew it! I knew I'd be found out! Oh, my God,
what'll I do?

RAFE *enters carrying a dust cover and a hanger.*

RAFE Mother, where's my new ... (*He sees the desk open
and places the cover and hanger on a chair.*) What
are you doing in my desk? Why is it open? What's
been happening? And my coat missing? What's
going on?

DAISY *runs into* RAFE'S *arms.*

DAISY Oh, Rafe – hold me tight.

RAFE I'll hold you, lass. There, there. Now, what's wrong?
Tell me all about it.

DAISY I can't. I can't bear to tell you.

RAFE Surely you can tell me anything?

DAISY I needed some money.

RAFE Go on.

DAISY And I got Betsy Jane to break the lock open for me.

RAFE (*moving to the desk*) You needed money – then why
didn't you come to me?

DAISY It was for our Hilda – she's going to London
tonight. But then your cash-box was locked and I
didn't know what to do. I got desperate – so I
pawned your overcoat instead. I had to get her
some money. I'm so sorry!

RAFE Why didn't you tell me?

DAISY I couldn't. Then when you caught me at the desk I
could see you looked so upset. Oh, Rafe ...

RAFE What happened to the housekeeping money?

DAISY (*sitting*) I wish I knew. Money has a funny way of
slipping through my fingers.

**RAFE**   Money has a funny way of slipping through
           anybody's fingers – if they keep 'em open.

**DAISY**  I lent Betsy Jane five pound last Friday. They'd
           come to take her television away, and she didn't
           pay me back.

**RAFE**   So she opened my desk as a return favour. You still
           haven't told me why you didn't come to me for the
           money in the first place.

**DAISY**  Because I wanted you to go on thinking I was a
           good manager. I knew if I asked I'd have to explain
           a lot and all my faults would come out. I'm not
           what you think I am – I'm a very poor manager.

**RAFE**   (*moving to* DAISY) Don't you realize that I love you
           for what you call your faults? I wouldn't want to
           change you for anything. As for your managing, I
           know more about that than you think. You wouldn't
           want two of my sort under one roof. I haven't made
           you go in fear of me, have I, lass?

**DAISY**  A bit. Your standards are too much for me. Over the
           weekend I got that I didn't know where to turn.

**RAFE**   It hurts me to hear you say that. It's the way my
           poor mother used to be and it's the one thing I was
           determined my wife would never be.

**DAISY**  Do try and forgive me, Dad.

**RAFE**   (*kissing* DAISY'S *forehead*) Nay, you must forgive me.
           I drove you to it. I try to do good by force, and
           force seems to blind a man. But the good you do,
           you do naturally, as though God were there with
           you.

**DAISY**  Don't say such things – you only upset me. Oh, but
           I'm so sorry about your lovely coat ...

**RAFE**   I don't care a bloody damn about the coat – or the
           desk – all I care about – all I've ever cared about –
           is you and our four children.

**DAISY**  I understand that.

**RAFE**   I know they don't thank me – but he'd be a poor
           father as went round looking for thanks from his
           children. A bit of love, happen, is as much as he

can expect – if he's lucky. (*He takes his savings book and an envelope from the desk.*) Our savings bank book, building society shares, ready cash for emergency. All this were here only for one purpose, so's we could pay our way in the world, and the family hold their heads up. Something I never knew in my childhood. Why, my poor mother hadn't a day's peace from bailiffs and tallymen. It was like a nightmare over the home. Every knock on our door was a threat. We daren't even answer it to a neighbour till we'd peeped through the curtains and made sure who it was.

DAISY  You never told me, Dad!

RAFE  It's not something a man wants to talk about. And I've never been one to seek pity. Going home from school I'd often spot a bailiff chap on the prowl. Then I'd have to sneak off and leave my mates and climb in over the backyard wall, making sure he wasn't following me. My mother would be waiting with a bundle of bedding to smuggle off to the pawnshop, or some scrap to take down to Aspinall's rag-and-bone yard. (*He sits in his chair.*) I reckon that's why I went off at Arthur last Friday when he brought up old Aspinall – it must have all come back to me.

DAISY  Yes, I felt there was something.

RAFE  Worst of all, she used to try and keep all her debts hidden from my dad and she'd tell him one lie to cover up another, and then want me to bear her out. He never knew where he was. And in the end he could stand it no longer and he left us.

DAISY  (*rising and moving to comfort* RAFE) Oh, Dad, I can't bear it.

RAFE  Now you know why I'm so obsessed about the truth. I know it's an obsession – but I just can't help it. I've never told you this before, but I came home from school one dinner-time and there were these two bailiff chaps sitting in our front room, playing cards, and when I went through into the back kitchen there was my mother – and she was trying to gas herself at the gas stove. That memory has never left my mind. I vowed that when I grew

up I'd never owe a halfpenny. It might seem little
enough to some folk to have paid their way, but I
can't tell you the peace of mind it has given me.
And whilst I might appear mindful of money, in my
heart I despise it. No matter how much I may have
to my name, the whole of it will never repay me
one iota of all the misery I once suffered – aye, and
those as were near me suffered – for the want of a
few paltry shillings.

DAISY   If only the children knew – I'm sure they'd
understand you better, Dad.

RAFE   (*rising*) Oh, no – I'm not begging to be understood
– not by my own flesh and blood. It'll come, in
time, when they have families of their own to bring
up. One night of tending a sick child will tell them
more of what they have meant to me than any
words of mine can. You have to go through your
own lot before you can make sense of it all. We're
none of us perfect, but we do our best. But I'll tell
you this, Mother – (*he sits and throws the savings
book and envelope down*) I'd sooner see this lot –
savings, security and everything – flung behind the
fire, rather than bring a moment's worry to you or
drive any one of our children from their own home.

DAISY   (*putting her arms round* RAFE) I know that, Dad, and
I've always known it. But I'll tell you what I think –
I think you might be happier from now on if you
just took us as God made us. The more you love
your children, the more you expect from them, and
they can't always live up to it. Neither can I.

RAFE *rises thoughtfully.*

RAFE   That reminds me, something's been troubling me all
weekend. It's about our Hilda. (*He paces up and
down.*)

DAISY *watches him.*

DAISY   What about her?

RAFE   She always loved fried herrings.

DAISY   Yes, as much as I do.

RAFE   Now think back – wasn't there a certain time when
you went off 'em?

DAISY   You don't mean ...?

RAFE   I mean when you were pregnant.

**DAISY** I could never face one then. But she can't be that way – not our Hilda! She's such an innocent.

**RAFE** I know she is, bless her. And I keep saying it can't be that. But there's some change come over her. What do you know, Mother?

**DAISY** I don't know anything. You can but guess in these days. I'll be honest – it has crossed my mind. But I've shut it out. Why, only this morning – but go on.

**RAFE** What about this morning?

**DAISY** Nothing.

**RAFE** Well, if she is like that – I'll see to it the child is born under my roof and not in some dump in London. Let's say no more about it. I'm ashamed of myself now, for how I've been with her.

**DAISY** In her heart she understands. But the trouble is, she's set on going to London tonight.

**RAFE** I'll have to put a stop to that.

**DAISY** But how?

**RAFE** You leave it to me. There's more ways of killing a pig than cutting its throat. Besides, I've a suspicion that they might all join forces – I can smell rebellion in the air – but I'll think of some stroke. You've got to protect the young from themselves. (*He detaches two keys from his ring.*) Here, you have these keys.

**DAISY** I don't really need them now, Dad, I can always turn to you.

**RAFE** I'd feel easier in my mind if you had them. I'd know for certain then you'd never be short.

**DAISY** (*taking the keys*) Thanks. And now I've something to live up to. Well, same as you say, let's not be too hasty about our Hilda. We don't know for sure.

**RAFE** You know nothing for sure in this life. You can only grope your way along, holding on to your bit of faith and putting on the best front possible.

WILFRED *and* HILDA *approach the front door, then hesitate and move away.*

DAISY    Well, you'd better put on a good one now, Dad, here they are.

RAFE     (*moving up stage*) Right – I'll see you.

DAISY    Are you going upstairs?

RAFE     I don't think I could face them – not right now.

DAISY    You'll have to face them – sooner or later.

RAFE     Will I?

DAISY    Don't lose heart. And remember what you've always said – never humble yourself before your children, or it makes them start doubting.

RAFE     (*picking up the dust cover and hanger*) I'll just go upstairs and rinse my face. And I'll remember that.

         RAFE *goes out.* DAISY *looks after him, then hurriedly turns to collect the savings book and other things.* HAROLD *approaches the front door.* DAISY *goes to the desk, puts the things inside, and locks it.* HAROLD *enters as she does so.*

HAROLD   What are you doing in his desk, Mum?

DAISY    Minding my own business.

         WILFRED *enters.*

WILFRED  I've been watching for him – where is he?

DAISY    Your father? He's upstairs. Why?

HAROLD   How come he's not going out?

WILFRED  Has he had a change of mind?

DAISY    He's had more than that...

WILFRED  Is it safe for 'em to come in?

DAISY    Is it their home, isn't it? When hasn't it been safe?

         WILFRED *and* HAROLD *react and look at each other.*

HAROLD   Wilf, tell 'em to come in.

         WILFRED *goes to the front door.*

         Are you sure you're all right, Mum?

DAISY    I think so. Why?

HAROLD   I don't know. I just wondered. You seem different. Oh, but wait till you hear our plans.

DAISY    What plans?

HAROLD   All right. Come on in, then.

FLORENCE, HILDA, ARTHUR *and* WILFRED *enter.* DAISY
*hurries across to hug* HILDA.

**HILDA**     Oh, Mum, are you all right?

**DAISY**     Ee, love, I'm so glad to see you.

FLORENCE *kisses* DAISY.

**FLORENCE**     Mother, we're bursting with news.

**ARTHUR**     Your Florence and I have decided to do it – at last.

WILFRED *closes the door and moves towards* HAROLD.

**WILFRED**     Do what?

**HAROLD**     (*giving* WILFRED *a push*) Get married, you nit! What
did you think?

**DAISY**     How nice!

**FLORENCE**     Wednesday morning, Mum, by special licence.

ARTHUR *gives* DAISY *a kiss on the cheek.*

**WILFRED**     D'you think it's worth it, Arthur?

**HAROLD**     Does he think what's worth it?

**WILFRED**     The extra expense of the licence.

**HAROLD**     He'll save that on the tax rebate.

**WILFRED**     I see – it might work out a bargain for him, together
with the foreman's job. You certainly know your
way about, Arthur.

**HAROLD**     (*giving* WILFRED *a push*); Shut up, Wilfred. Know
what – Mum – our Hilda's not going to London.

**HILDA**     No, but I'm not staying at home. I've arranged to go
and stay with Betty Partington until I get things
sorted out.

**WILFRED**     Well, keep your suitcase locked in that household.

**HAROLD**     Wilf, stop butting in! And break our news to Mum.

**WILFRED**     What news? Oh, yes – we've all planned to leave
home.

**HAROLD**     Aye, we're getting out at last, Mum.

**DAISY**     (*sitting in* RAFE'S *chair*) Why not? Home's the place
you can always  come back to when nobody else
wants you.

**FLORENCE**     (*moving to* DAISY) And we're all set for you to come
and live with Arthur and me – after what happened
yesterday.

**DAISY**     I've stood thirty years of yesterdays, love – one sort

|            | or another. Now what about your dad? What's been arranged for him? |
|------------|---|
| **WILFRED** | We never gave him a thought. |
| **DAISY** | Never gave your dad a thought ...? |
| **HAROLD** | Let him have the blooming house to himself – see how he gets on then. |
| **HILDA** | Don't talk like that about leaving Dad alone – in spite of what he drove you to, Mum. |
| **DAISY** | What do you mean, drove me to? |
| **HILDA** | Betsy Jane told me on the quiet – how you had to pawn his new overcoat. |
| **DAISY** | Sssh – sssh! |
| **HAROLD** | His thirty-two guinea overcoat in pop! I don't believe it! |
| **WILFRED** | You haven't really put it in uncle's! |
| **DAISY** | Yes, I had to. I needed the money for our Hilda, and I'd nowhere to turn. |
| **WILFRED** | Just fancy, and we were yapping away for him to put it on. |
| **HAROLD** | *You* were! |
| **FLORENCE** | Does he know? |
| **DAISY** | Yes, I told him everything. |
|            | *They look at one another in wonder.* |
| **HAROLD** | He'll never come down them stairs alive. |
| **HILDA** | What did he say, Mum? |
| **FLORENCE** | What did he say! |
| **DAISY** | I'll tell you what he said. He said he was sorry and asked me to forgive him. |
| **HAROLD** | By heck, he must have changed a hell of a lot in the last five minutes – if he said forgive me! |
|            | *There is a knock at the front door.* |
| **WILFRED** | Somebody at door, Harold. |
|            | HAROLD *starts to move up to open the door, caught unaware in the moment of confusion. Then he raises his fist at* WILFRED *for having caught him, and continues his move to door.* |

DAISY    And what's more, he gave me these. (*She holds up the keys.*)

WILFRED    The keys to his desk?

FLORENCE    He didn't, did he?

HILDA    I don't believe it.

HAROLD *enters with* BETSY JANE.

BETSY JANE    It's only me.

DAISY    What is it, Betsy Jane?

BETSY JANE    (*dipping into her handbag*)Yon fellow had a big win on the horses – he's just come home drunk, and I've been through his pockets already. So here's two pounds off what I owe you. Pay your debts and you can come again.

HAROLD    You haven't paid 'em yet.

WILFRED    Don't forget there's another three quid.

BETSY JANE    You shut up. Here you are, Daisy.

DAISY    No, thanks.

BETSY JANE    What's up?

HAROLD    She wants all or nothing.

DAISY    I don't want to touch the money.

HAROLD    Have you gone out of your mind, Mum?

*The others murmur in surprise.*

DAISY    No! But on one condition – that you never come to me to borrow another ha'penny.

HAROLD    But five pounds, Mum!

WILFRED    She might never see the other three.

FLORENCE    It's a lot of money just the same.

DAISY    It'll have been worth it for the change it's brought my life.

FLORENCE    (*rising*) But, Mother ...

ARTHUR    (*cutting in*) I see your mother's point. She wants her peace of mind. So let her have it.

DAISY    That's it, Arthur.

BETSY JANE    Of course, if you'd rather not take it, I understand. (*Quickly returning the money to her bag.*) It'll mean

|           | I'll have to find another neighbour to tap – because I'll never have the nerve to come to you again. |
|-----------|------|
| WILFRED   | You'll get the dirty kick-out if you do. |
| HILDA     | You keep out of it – you won't be here. |
| WILFRED   | How do you mean – I won't be here? |
| HAROLD    | You're leaving home, didn't you know? |
| WILFRED   | Oh, I'd forgot! |
| BETSY JANE | Ee, Florence, I think it's a crying shame things should have come to this pass for your poor mother – the entire family going at one swoop. Still, I'd love to see your father's face when he gets home from his Hallelujah Chorus. |
| HAROLD    | He's not gone. |
| BETSY JANE | Then where the hell is he – out on the booze? |
| ARTHUR    | Mr Crompton's upstairs. |
| BETSY JANE | Upstairs! Sufferin' Alice! Why didn't somebody warn me? I'm off! Excuse me, everybody, but I don't want to meet him. I might tell him a few home truths. *(She hurries to the door.)* RAFE *enters as* BETSY JANE *reaches it.* BETSY JANE, *waving behind her, does not see him, until she turns and collides with him.* Oh – Mr Crompton – I do beg your pardon – I – I'm just off ... RAFE *looks at her keenly, then stoops to pick up a hairpin.* |
| RAFE      | Hy, just a tick, missis – you've dropped something. |
| BETSY JANE | It's only a hairpin. |
| RAFE      | Aye, but you never know when you might need it. Here y'are. Good night – and go careful now. BETSY JANE *takes the hairpin and stares, fascinated, at* RAFE *as she goes out speechless.* RAFE *comes down, approaching the silent group.* ARTHUR *looks to the others for someone to speak.* |
| ARTHUR    | *(getting no help)* She's a rum 'un. |
| RAFE      | Aren't we all – in our different ways. Arthur, I've been thinking over some of those things you said to me yesterday tea-time. |
| ARTHUR    | *(moving to* RAFE*)* So have I. Did I overstep the mark? |

RAFE    Nay, never regret having spoken your mind. I only
        wish I'd done it more often.
        HAROLD *and* WILFRED *react.*

ARTHUR  Oh! Me an' your ... your Florence and I thought of
        getting married.

FLORENCE  (*putting her arm through* ARTHUR'S) Thought! We are!

ARTHUR  Oh, aye – sorry, Flo – Wednesday morning – by
        special licence.

RAFE    It shouldn't be a rush job, but as St Paul says, it's
        better to marry than to burn. Mother, find out the
        number of guests and go down to the Co-op
        restaurant first thing in the morning. Order the best
        breakfast they do. Don't mind the cost, Arthur. I can
        pay for it.

ARTHUR  No, I'm sorry – you can't – I mean we aren't –
        Florence ...!

FLORENCE  We aren't thinking of getting married from here, Dad.

RAFE    Why – where else would you get married from, lass
        – but your own home?

DAISY   She thought of getting married from Arthur's
        mother's.

RAFE    Did she? Well, she can't.

ARTHUR  What do you mean, Mr Crompton – 'she can't'?

RAFE    (*patting* ARTHUR *on the shoulder*) Listen, Arthur,
        you've won one round – don't let it go to your
        head. You don't have a bride and groom going out
        of the same front door, and travelling in the same
        cab to their wedding, do you?

ARTHUR  I hadn't thought of that.

RAFE    (*to* FLORENCE) And do you realize the years your
        mother must have looked forward to this occasion –
        to the day she'd see her eldest daughter go out that
        door a bride?

DAISY   Our Florence had planned to stay these next nights
        at Arthur's.

RAFE    Our Florence can't stay these next nights at Arthur's.
        One night away from home is quite enough before
        marriage. You don't want to go making a habit of it.

FLORENCE  (*moving to* DAISY *and taking her hand*) Of course,
Arthur, if Dad thinks it's the proper thing to do – to
marry from here ...

ARTHUR  Aye, well yes, it will save us moving your bags ...

RAFE  Is there anything else, Mother, while we're about it?
(*He nods to* DAISY, *indicating* HILDA.)

DAISY  (*rising*) Our Hilda –
HILDA *rises.*
– I think we must tell your dad now – (*moving
towards* HILDA) she's set on leaving home.

RAFE  Leave home, eh? What a wonderful thought! I envy
you.

HAROLD  She's not the only one going.
RAFE *turns slowly.*
I'm going an' all. (*Nudging* WILFRED.) And him.

WILFRED  Oh? What? Yes!

HAROLD  And we're going tonight.

RAFE  You know something – you should have done it
years ago. Think of the freedom! How I envy you
all! I only wish I could leave home – just like that.
What do you say, Mother?

DAISY  It must be nice – having the choice.

HILDA  (*crossing below* DAISY) I'll just go upstairs and
collect the rest of my things. (*She moves towards the
door.*)

RAFE  (*stopping her*) I'll miss you, love – I'll miss all of you
– but I don't blame you. The times I've reached that
top corner on my way home from work and have
thought to myself, if only I had the guts to turn the
other way – to get away from it all, start life afresh
somewhere. But I've always lacked the courage.

WILFRED  (*accusingly*) You never wanted to leave us, did you,
Dad?
*The others stiffen.*

RAFE  I'm only human – I wasn't born married. Why, I was
only thinking last Friday tea-time as I came through
that door – there'll be our Harold taking the mickey,
our Hilda in one of her moods, and there'll be

Mother, bless her, with that frozen look of honesty she puts on her face after the last-minute fiddling of the housekeeping accounts. Florence, I don't know what it'll be like now that you're going.

**DAISY** Oh, Dad, don't say you knew all the time!

**RAFE** Over the years I've hardly been able to keep a straight face going through your figures. Know what the window-cleaning has cost this past month? Two pounds fourteen and ninepence! It's a wonder there's any glass left!

**DAISY** It's a pity after keeping quiet all this time you had to come out with it just now.

**RAFE** Well, we were all putting a front on, weren't we? But now we've got to put our house in order, so in the future let's have no more secrets from one another. Out with everything.

**HAROLD** O.K., I'll make a start now. (*He deliberately lights a cigarette.*)

**DAISY** Dad, I think you'd better take your keys back.

**RAFE** Why? What for?

**DAISY** I feel I'm not cut out for cashier. I'm a rotten reckoner.

**RAFE** But you're in sole charge now. You won't have to reckon – you'll just have to spend. You've nobody to answer to but yourself.

**DAISY** Oh, yes, I'd forgot – and there'll only be the one pay packet every Friday. It'll be easy.(*She smiles at the doleful faces.*) No borrowing, no lending – with just two mouths to feed.

**WILFRED** And the cat! Don't forget him.

**RAFE** He'll not go hungry.

**DAISY** (*dangling the keys*) Well, if you change your mind …

**RAFE** Nay, I'm not likely to – I've come to realize that anything you have to lock away with a key just isn't worth the worry. And, same as they say, the home will be here when we're gone. I'll go and get my coat.

**DAISY** Why – you're not going out, are you?

**RAFE** I thought you might like to say goodbye to one another in peace.

**WILFRED** You're not in our way, Dad. Is he?

ARTHUR    No – not at all.

RAFE    (*moving towards* WILFRED) Thanks, lad, very good of you, I'm sure. But I need some fresh air. And I dare say you've a lot to talk over. (*He stops in front of* HAROLD *and looks at the cigarette.*)
HAROLD *reacts with nervous bravado.* RAFE *is unexpectedly gentle .*
Forgetting your manners, son? Pass them round, can't you?
RAFE *goes out for his coat.*

WILFRED    You heard what he said!
WILFRED *and* ARTHUR *go to get their cigarettes from* HAROLD. HAROLD *stubs his cigarette out.*

WILFRED    What's up?

HAROLD    I didn't like the way he said it. What's come over him, Mum?

ARTHUR    (*rejoining* FLORENCE) He seems quite different.

WILFRED    Aye, he's not like his normal self.

HAROLD    I never knew he had one.

WILFRED    I've a feeling he's up to something.

HILDA    I think it's very irresponsible of him to pick a time like this to go out – with so much to be settled.

FLORENCE    Oh, you shut up – you caused it all.

HILDA    Me!

FLORENCE    Why didn't you eat that bloody herring!
*They all look at* FLORENCE *in astonishment.* HILDA *sits.* RAFE *enters with his coat and cap.*

RAFE    Mother, do you remember the morning we got married?

DAISY    Yes, I'll never forget it. I can see you this minute, standing at the altar at St Philip's Church, and the organ playing. Why?

RAFE    You'd never have imagined then, with all the years ahead, and being blessed by a family, that the time would come when they all suddenly clear off and leave you over a single weekend. And that we'd end up all on our own, more or less the same as we started.

DAISY    Aye, except a flamin' sight older, uglier – and wiser!

RAFE    I only hope it never happens to any of you. It can be a nasty wrench.

*The others appear affected by this.* RAFE *moves to* ARTHUR *and shakes his hand, then goes to kiss* FLORENCE *and wish her luck, then out to the hall. Meanwhile,* DAISY *moves to between* FLORENCE *and* HAROLD.

DAISY    Somebody's got to stop him going out.

HAROLD    Why?

DAISY    Your father's not himself. Anything could happen.

WILFRED    Aye, he might never come back. He could go from one extreme to the other. They do, y'know – his sort. And you heard what he said about wanting to leave us all in the lurch.

HAROLD    You leave it to me, Mum. I'll put the block on him.

RAFE    (*beckoning to* DAISY *as he is about to go*) Mother, I'm off ...

HAROLD *goes to the door.*

HAROLD    Just a moment, Father.

RAFE    What is it?

HAROLD    I'd like a word with you.

RAFE    What about?

HAROLD    About this upheaval.

WILFRED    Which upheaval?

HAROLD    Blimey, have you forgotten again? You're leaving home!

WILFRED    Sorry – it had slipped my mind.

HAROLD    How many more times do I have to tell you?

ARTHUR    Don't forget you'll both have to find lodgings for the night.

WILFRED    So we shall.

HAROLD    Lodgings! That side of it never struck me!

WILFRED    Why, did you think we could walk the streets all night?

RAFE    (*to* HAROLD) You were saying?

HAROLD    One moment, Father...

WILFRED    (*to* HAROLD) Do you know anybody who'll take us in?

HAROLD    How should I know? I've never been a vagrant. Do you know anybody, Mum?

DAISY    No, love, I don't. Ask your dad.

| | |
|---|---|
| **HAROLD** | (*beckoning*) Wilf ... |
| **WILFRED** | Dad, you don't know anybody who'd take me and our Harold in, do you? |
| **RAFE** | No, not just like that. They nearly all want references these days. 'Course your mother would give you one. What were you after – full board, bed and breakfast, or just your kip for the night? |
| | WILFRED *and* HAROLD *look at each other bewildered.* |
| **WILFRED** | I never knew it was such a business. |
| **DAISY** | I suppose at a pinch they could get in at the Salvation Army hostel. |
| **RAFE** | Aye, they're not too particular. |
| **ARTHUR** | Ee, I don't think they'd like it there. |
| **RAFE** | Not to worry – they'll find something. |
| **FLORENCE** | I just can't imagine the home without our Wilf and Harold. |
| | WILFRED *looks sad.* |
| **ARTHUR** | Aye, they were like fixtures, so the place is bound to seem empty. |
| **WILFRED** | (*to* HAROLD) Well, come on, it's getting late. And we've nothing packed yet. |
| **HAROLD** | Now you don't want to be rash, Wilfred... |
| **WILFRED** | Me – rash! How do you mean? |
| **HAROLD** | It's all right making your bid for freedom – but you've got to think of Mother and the home. You were born in this house. Remember? |
| **WILFRED** | No, I don't! |
| **RAFE** | (*to* HAROLD) You were saying? |
| **HAROLD** | Yes, Father, I've been thinking things over. What say we all hung on and gave it another go – pull together, like? |
| **ARTHUR** | Good idea – bury the hatchet! |
| **WILFRED** | I'm willing – if everybody else is. |
| | WILFRED *and* HAROLD *brighten up.* |
| **FLORENCE** | Yes, it seems such a pity to split up. |

| | |
|---|---|
| **WILFRED** | Aye, especially at a time like this – just when we're getting to know each other. |
| **HAROLD** | What do you say, Mum? |
| **DAISY** | Your dad and I have no choice. It's all been the one go for us ever since our family came along. Eh, Dad? |
| **RAFE** | Aye, you're tied to your children – even if they're not to you. But now I feel it's all come to an end. |
| | *The others murmur in surprise.* |
| **HAROLD** | How do you mean? |
| **FLORENCE** | In what way? |
| **RAFE** | It wouldn't work any more. I've come to see our Hilda was right |
| **WILFRED** | How? |
| **RAFE** | A home can become a prison where there isn't love. |
| **HILDA** | (*rising*) I never meant it like that. |
| **DAISY** | Of course she didn't. |
| **RAFE** | No matter how well it's run. |
| **FLORENCE** | You've got it wrong, Dad. |
| **RAFE** | Nay, I must have failed you. Sorry. God bless, everybody. (*He turns to the door.*) I'm off. |
| **HILDA** | I tell you I didn't mean it that way! |
| **HAROLD** | Now steady up, Dad. (*He detains* RAFE.) Don't be too hasty. |
| **ARTHUR** | Love, Mr Crompton – why, there's any God's amount of love in this house! Even I can see that. |
| **WILFRED** | 'Course there is. |
| **FLORENCE** | (*putting her arm through* ARTHUR'S) Always has been. |
| **DAISY** | Surely you knew that, Dad? |
| **RAFE** | Well, I've had my doubts of late. |
| **WILFRED** | I'm not suprised. |
| | HAROLD *digs* WILFRED *to shut up.* |
| **HAROLD** | It's just that we've a funny way of showing it. |
| **WILFRED** | Aye, that's it. |
| **DAISY** | Happen we're a funny lot. |
| | RAFE *surveys them.* |

RAFE    Yes, I see what you mean.

DAISY    But when you get down to it, what family isn't?

WILFRED    And it's a poor home that won't stand the odd row.

HAROLD    Shut up! (*He takes* RAFE's *cap and coat.*) Well, now the air's been cleared, what say we stick around and have another bash – eh, Wilf?

WILFRED    I suppose we could go farther and fare worse.

DAISY    You could, for sure. (*Crossing to* RAFE.) But what about you, Dad?

RAFE    You know me. I'm easy. Will somebody put the kettle on?

WILFRED    Harold, the kettle!

HAROLD *turns towards the kitchen, then catches on and raises his fist at* WILFRED.

HILDA    Dad ...!

HILDA *walks towards* RAFE, *as —*

*The* CURTAIN *falls*

# QUESTIONS AND EXPLORATIONS

## 1 Keeping Track

The questions in this section are designed to help your reading and understanding of the play in the areas of plot, character, structure and interaction. They may be used as you read the play or afterwards, for discussion or for writing. Some are developed in the *Explorations* section.

*Act One*

1 What do we learn about the nature of the Crompton family from the opening stage directions?

2 How effective is Daisy in dealing with the housekeeping money?

3 How would the character of Betsy Jane behave in the Crompton house?

4 What impression of Rafe does the audience start to form?

5 Why does Daisy react to what Betsy Jane says?

6 What is the nature of the relationship between Wilfred and Harold?

7 From whom is Hilda expecting a letter?

8 What attitudes do Florence, Wilfred and Harold have towards their father?

9 What is the atmosphere in the house before Rafe's arrival?

10 How does it change with his return home?

11  How would the character of Rafe be portrayed?

12  How do the members of the family react to Rafe?

13  What does the way Rafe collects the housekeeping money show us about the family?

14  How are meals conducted in the Crompton household?

15  Why does Rafe challenge Hilda over the herring?

16  How do the other members of the family react?

17  And how does Hilda react? Why?

18  What does the episode with Rafe's new coat reveal?

19  How would the character of Arthur be portrayed?

20  How does Rafe's presence affect the others?

21  How do the members of the family react to Arthur's news?

22  How does it change the atmosphere in the room?

23  Why does Rafe hold such strong opinions about Alf Aspinall?

24  How does the atmosphere change with Rafe's departure?

25  What is Arthur's attitude to Rafe?

26  What has Arthur noticed about Hilda?

27  What would the audience's reaction be to the climax of Act One?

## Act Two: Scene One

1  How is the appearance of the room changed?

2  How far has the situation between Hilda and Rafe progressed?

3  How has it affected the household as a whole?

4  Why has Hilda decided to eat the herring?

5 And why has Rafe decided not to make her eat it?

6 What is Rafe's attitude in raising his children?

7 How would Wilfred behave in dealing with the herring?

8 How would the family react to the news that the herring has gone?

9 How would Rafe behave in questioning the family?

10 And how would they react to his questioning?

11 Why does Rafe pursue Wilfred so far?

12 How would the family react to this?

13 Why does Hilda leave?

14 What makes Arthur stand up to Rafe?

15 Why does Florence decide to leave with Arthur?

16 How do the various members of the family, including Rafe, react to her going?

*Act Two: Scene Two*

1 How is the appearance of the room changed?

2 How would Daisy show her reaction to Betsy Jane?

3 How would Hilda enter?

4 Why does Daisy react when Hilda says she felt sick?

5 What is Daisy's attitude to living with Rafe?

6 Why has Hilda decided to leave home for good?

7 What is Betsy Jane's attitude to men?

8 Why does Daisy prevent Betsy Jane from breaking into the cash-box?

9 Why does she allow Betsy Jane to take Rafe's new coat to the pawnbroker?

*Act Two: Scene Three*

1  What is the atmosphere in the room at the start of the scene?

2  How is the family, including Rafe, affected by Florence and Hilda's absence?

3  Why is Harold so keen that Rafe should go into Manchester?

4  How would Daisy react to Wilfred suggesting Rafe wears his new overcoat?

5  How is Daisy behaving?

6  How does Rafe react to Daisy's confessions?

7  What do we learn about Rafe's attitude to himself?

8  And what do we learn about his early life?

9  How do Rafe and Daisy feel towards each other?

10  What are the Crompton children's various plans?

11  Why does Daisy refuse Betsy Jane's repayment?

12  How do the Crompton children react to Rafe's new attitude?

13  How does the atmosphere in the family start to change?

14  Why do Wilfred and Harold decide not to leave?

15  How would an audience react to the play's conclusion?

# 2 Explorations

The questions in this section are more detailed and rely on your having read the whole play. Some of the questions develop ideas from the *Keeping Track* section. Because they tend to be more detailed, they offer the opportunity to develop the ideas into written, oral or practical coursework assignments. Some will require a close knowledge of the play; others will require a more imaginative response.

## A Characters

*Rafe Crompton*

1 'How can a man run a home? That's the woman's job, always has been'. How does Rafe run the Crompton home?

2 'I don't need livening up'. What are the qualities that Rafe Crompton most prizes?

3 'Well, there's nobody taking me for granted'. What are Rafe's priorities in bringing up his family?

4 'Poor Dad, always on his own'. How is Rafe seen by the other members of his family?

5 'You know me. I'm easy'. How easy is Rafe to live with? Give examples from the play.

6 If Rafe kept a diary, what would he write in it after Act Two, Scene One and after Act Two, Scene Three?

*Daisy*

7 'But a mother has to keep these feelings to herself'. What are Daisy's feelings and reactions as the events of the play progress?

8 'Life's not been easy for you, Mum, with him'. How has Daisy been able to live with Rafe?

9 'Your standards are too much for me'. What are the standards by which Daisy has to live?

10 'The more you love your children, the more you expect from them, and they can't always live up to it'. What are Daisy's priorities in raising the family?

11 If Daisy kept a diary, what would she write in it at the end of Act Two, Scene One and at the end of Act Two, Scene Three?

## Hilda

12 'I don't know what's come over our Hilda lately'. Can you account for Hilda's behaviour during the course of the play?

13 'They say the apple doesn't fall far from the tree'. In what ways is Hilda similar to her father?

14 'Open confession is good for the soul'. What and how would Hilda have told Betsy Jane on the night she spent with her?

15 If Hilda kept a diary, what would she write in it at the end of Act Two, Scene One and at the end of Act Two, Scene Three?

## Florence

16 'Your sister Flo is father-fixated'. What does Harold mean by this? Is he correct?

17 'I can only be as I am'. Can you account for Florence's reactions during the course of the play?

18 If Florence kept a diary, what would she write in it at the end of Act Two, Scene One and at the end of Act Two, Scene Three?

## Harold and Wilfred

19 'Let him come to me if he has any complaints and I'll tell him where he gets off'. What are the sons' attitudes to their father? Is there any difference between them?

20 'I wouldn't do a thing like that, Dad'. Why does Wilfred give the herring to the cat? What did he hope to achieve?

21 'What say we all hung on and gave it another go, pull together, like?' What do the sons hope to gain from the events of the play?

## Arthur and Betsy Jane

22 'They're always talking about you and him and his domineering ways'. What is the function of Betsy Jane within the play? What are her attitudes to Daisy and to Rafe?

23 'Don't be so liberal with your advice. You're not a member of the family yet'. What is the function of Arthur within the play? What are his attitudes to Rafe, Florence and to the family?

## General

24 Create and write a scene that shows the following Friday's tea-time. Using your understanding of the characters, imagine and create their new understandings of each other. Pay attention to dialogue, interaction and characterisation to show if/how the family's life has changed.

25 Select one member of the Crompton family. Write a monologue for your selected character in which they reflect upon the events of the play and their effects upon the family. Pay attention to characterisation and expression in showing how, if at all, they have been changed by these events. How will you want an audience to react to your character's speech?

## B  Themes

1  'If your children once beat you, you're licked for good'.
   What are the standards that have been applied in
   raising the Crompton children? How successful have
   their parents been in raising them?

2  'Money can be a good servant but a very poor master'.
   How is money (mis)managed in the play? What morals
   are we intended to draw?

3  'Well, we were all putting a front on, weren't we?' What
   are the effects of the various 'fronts' that are put on by
   the members of the family?

4  'A home can be a prison where there isn't love'. What
   makes a happy home in Naughton's opinion?

5  'We're none of us perfect, but we do our best'. What is
   an audience intended to learn from witnessing the
   events of the play?

## C  In Performance

1  Select one of the scenes from the play. Using the stage
   directions in Act One and at the start of your selected
   scene, draw up a set design brief. What set, furniture
   and props would be required? How would you dress
   the set to convey the atmosphere Naughton intends to
   the audience?

2  Select one of the members of the Crompton family.
   What aspects of that character would you need as an
   actor to highlight in performance for the benefit of an
   audience? How would you use voice, gesture and
   movement to achieve this?

3  Show how the actor playing Rafe Crompton could
   show the developing nature of the character in the
   course of a performance.

4  Select one of the climaxes from the play (the Friday tea

scene or the inquisition of Wilfred, for example).
Suggest how this extract could be directed, for the
benefit of an audience, to show the full drama of the
situation. Refer to speech, movement, reaction and
interaction as appropriate.

5 As a director of the play, what would you wish to
highlight for the benefit of the audience? Explain how
you would endeavour to achieve this.

6 Design a poster advertising a production of the play for
your local theatre. How will you interest and attract a
potential audience? What other publicity would you
require in order to make the play a success? What form
would this take?

## D Criticism

1 'Naughton's Bolton is an old-fashioned and sometimes
sentimentally conceived place' (Ian Watson). How far is
this true in *Spring and Port Wine*?

2 Naughton's writing displays 'an understanding of his
characters which gives them the stamp of authenticity'
(Alan Strachan). How successfully does Naughton
create the characters of *Spring and Port Wine*? How is
this achieved?

3 Naughton is concerned to present the 'basic truth of
human behaviour' (Strachan). What are the basic truths
he presents to the audience in *Spring and Port Wine*?

4 *Spring and Port Wine* finishes with 'a contrived happy
ending of reconciliation' (Strachan). How successfully
and effectively does Naughton resolve the problems
created by his characters in the play?

5 Naughton's work is distinguished by its attention to
detail. How is the Cromptons' family life conveyed to
the audience? How successful is Naughton in his
creation of the family?